contents

Written by Frank Connolly & Dr Ronan Lynch
Research: Dr Ronan Lynch
Photography: Derek Speirs (except where indicated)
Design: Public Communications Centre
Printed by: Hudson Killeen

Published by:
Centre for Public Inquiry-Fiosrú an Phobail
The Courtyard, 25 Great Strand Street, Dublin 1
Tel: 01 8748851   Fax: 01 8748976
E mail: info@publicinquiry.ie
Website: www.publicinquiry.ie
CPI Logo: Robert Ballagh

EXECUTIVE SUMMARY

1 The Corrib gas field, which is controlled by a consortium including Shell (45%), the Norwegian state company Statoil (36.5%) and Marathon (18.5%), is worth up to €8 billion according to sources in the oil and gas industry. Its discovery was announced in 1996. The Corrib and associated fields in the Slyne/Erris basin off the north west coast of Ireland are estimated to be worth up to €50 billion. Through Statoil, the Norwegian tax payer benefits more directly from the gas find than the Irish public. Following the introduction of a new fiscal and licensing regime for the industry in 1987 and 1992, the Irish tax payer receives no royalties from the find while development costs can be written off against tax.

2 Changes to the 1975 fiscal and licensing terms are weighed heavily in favour of the oil and gas companies. While designed to encourage exploration and drilling the record shows that the new terms introduced by former minister, Ray Burke, in 1987 and then finance minister, Bertie Ahern, in 1992 had little effect in this regard and effectively ceded control of vast offshore reserves to the oil and gas industry.

3 In 1987, Mr Burke exempted the oil and gas industry from royalty payments and abolished all State participation in the commercial development of important natural resources. He introduced a 100% tax write off against profits on capital expenditure for exploration, development and production for up to 25 years.

4 In 1992, then Minister for Finance, Bertie Ahern, reduced Corporation Tax on oil and gas companies from 50% to 25%. The 1992 licensing terms allowed the oil and gas companies to secure licences covering extensive offshore areas for long periods of time with minimal drilling requirements.

5 A proposal in the 1970s to establish an Irish State company to develop the country's oil and gas resources and offers by the Norwegian government to assist in its creation were rejected by the Irish government at the time. When, in 1979, a state company, the Irish National Petroleum Corporation, was set up to guarantee oil supplies during an emergency it was explicitly prohibited from any involvement in exploration and drilling.

6 In 2002, the Irish government introduced statutory instruments into legislation which allow the Minister for Communications, Marine and Natural Resources to make Compulsory Acquisition Orders for the benefit of private companies which permit them to acquire land without the permission of property owners. Five men from County Mayo spent 94 days in jail during 2005 when they refused to permit Shell E&P to exercise these orders.

7 The Government also introduced legislation to allow the department to grant permission for an upstream pipeline, carrying untreated gas, without it being subject to normal planning procedures.

8 Following public hearings in 2002 a senior inspector of An Bord Pleanála rejected the proposed location for a gas processing plant at Ballinaboy Bridge in County Mayo. Mr Kevin Moore stated that the proposed plant was in the wrong location and upheld the appeal by local residents against planning permission. In his decision he cited the threat to a sensitive and scenic location, the instability associated with the removal of hundreds of thousands of tonnes of peat bog and the risk of a major accident.

9 In 2003, senior executives of Shell E&P were granted a meeting with the Taoiseach, Bertie Ahern, the former Minister for Communications, Marine and Natural Resources, Dermot Ahern and former Minister for the Environment, Martin Cullen and senior government officials to express their concerns over planning delays.

10 Within a week representatives of the consortium seeking to develop the Corrib gas field were granted a meeting with the chairman of An Bord Pleanála, John O'Connor, and members of the planning appeals board to discuss their concerns.

11 In 2004, the Shell-led consortium was granted planning permission after altering their original proposal to dump hundreds of thousands of tonnes of peat near the intended gas processing plant and instead remove it to a site some 11 kilometres away at Bangor Erris.

12 The Department of Communications, Marine and Natural Resources failed to properly supervise work by Shell E&P which erected a section of the controversial pipeline without the necessary ministerial consents. They were subsequently forced to dismantle it.

13 The Department also commissioned a safety review of the proposed pipeline, which was originally routed through an area affected by landslides, from a company which was part owned by Shell and was forced to commission an alternative review after public protest.

14 A safety review commissioned by the Centre for Public Inquiry from US company, Accufacts Inc. has found that the current proposed route of the pipeline is unacceptable and that claims that it meets "the highest international standards" are meaningless. The report raises serious questions concerning the credibility of the current proposal and also concludes that the benefits of locating the gas processing plant offshore have not been properly addressed.

15 In the latest round of licences issued in August 2005, frontier licences were allocated to a Shell-led consortium and to Island Oil and Gas, an Irish based company. Providence Resources, controlled by Tony O'Reilly, the owner of Independent News and Media, is the largest Irish company involved in offshore oil and gas activity and controls significant acreages off the west coast and in the Celtic Sea.

16 The Government has stated on several occasions that the benefit to Ireland from the Corrib gas field will be to increase the attractiveness of the northwest as an investment location; the creation of jobs in construction and operation of the connector pipeline and processing plant and to ensure 'security of supply' and reduce reliance on gas from 'unstable' regions of the world.

The Proposed Corrib Onshore System An Independent Analysis

by Richard Kuprewicz
President, Accufacts Inc.

KEY FINDINGS

- The Corrib pipeline is not a "normal" pipeline given its potential to operate under exotically high pressures and because of the unknown gas compositions associated with gas field production. This can seriously increase the likelihood of pipe failure.

- The Quantified Risk Assessment (QRA) is inappropriate for this highly unique, first of its kind, pipeline as there is no historical data that can be used to evaluate this proposed system.

- The route of the pipeline, as currently proposed, is unacceptable because of its close proximity to people and dwellings.

- The thick-walled pipe is not invincible to leak or rupture from the expected high pressures and the destructive potential of reactive gases.

- There are too many unknowns regarding the future operation of this pipeline - especially in the areas of gas pressure and gas composition that can lead to failure.

- Maximum pipeline pressure, a condition that should be easily defined, has not been clearly demonstrated or documented - a grave deficiency.

- This pipeline's uniquely large rupture impact zone with high fatalities raises many questions about the appropriateness of the current proposal and QRA approaches.

- Claims of meeting "highest international standards" are meaningless as no standard adequately addresses the numerous issues associated with this unique proposal.

- Routing analyses for the onshore systems are seriously deficient while the difficulties with locating the gas processing plant offshore are overstated.

- This report raises critical questions concerning the credibility of the current proposal, and should call into question the validity of evaluations concerning this project.

101
242

introduction

The recent discovery of rich deposits of natural gas off the west coast of Ireland, and the manner in which a consortium led by the global conglomerate, Royal Dutch Shell, intends to bring the gas onshore, has generated a renewed debate over the control of the country's oil and gas resources.

LOCAL PROTEST, NATIONAL DEBATE

More immediately it has also focused national and international attention on a remote, rural community in northwest Mayo that has expressed deep concern over the threat to its health and safety arising from the route of the proposed pipeline to carry untreated gas from deep Atlantic waters 80 kilometres off the Erris peninsula.

The imprisonment of five residents of Ros Dumhach (Rossport) and surrounding areas in the Mayo Gaeltacht for 94 days for refusing to obey a High Court order forbidding them from obstructing the planned pipeline has turned a local environmental controversy into a national dispute that has polarised attitudes and renewed public debate over the relationship between successive governments and powerful international oil companies.

A detailed examination of that relationship has raised serious questions about decisions made over several decades by administrations torn between the need to explore and develop lucrative and vital national resources and the desire to maintain sovereign control over strategically important oil and gas fields. As the world supply of hydrocarbons rapidly depletes, and oil and gas prices escalate, the political decisions made over the past 30 years are now under public scrutiny like never before.

With the benefit of hindsight it is arguable that the terms and conditions under which the oil and gas companies operate in Ireland are over-generous and that the repeated concessions to the demands of the some of the world's most powerful financial interests were ill advised and premature.

FROM PROTECTION TO GIVE-AWAY

The agreement with Marathon Oil in 1960, the 1975 Offshore Licensing Terms, the 1992 Offshore Licensing Terms and the 1992 Finance Act are the principal regimes governing the oil and gas industry in Ireland.

From a position in 1975 when senior civil servants devised licensing and fiscal terms which ensured substantial state participation in any oil and gas production, significant royalties on production and a vigorous taxation regime, the Irish State has effectively removed most, if not all, of the constraints imposed on the oil and gas multinationals.

Underlying the decisions which permitted this erosion of State involvement in the exploitation of the nation's natural resources was an undoubted desire to ensure that the economic climate was created to facilitate the expensive exploration process in technologically challenging conditions off the western seaboard.

Changes in 1985 and 1987 were to provide a kick start for oil exploration but the 1992 terms placed almost all control over the resources into the hands of the oil companies.

MINISTER JUSTIN KEATING'S VISION

In 1975, officials in the Department of Industry and Commerce prepared draft terms for offshore exploration on behalf of the then minister, Justin Keating. He was heavily influenced by the manner in which the Norwegian government had sought to develop its indigenous oil and gas resources in the face of stiff opposition from the oil majors.

He and his colleagues in government were also highly critical of the terms agreed by a previous Fianna Fáil government with Marathon Oil for the development of the Kinsale gas fields.

The 1975 terms included a provision for the State to acquire a 50% maximum stake in any commercial find, production royalties of between 8% and 16% and production bonuses on significant finds. The standard corporation tax of 50% was also applied, while the terms sought to commit

companies to a programme that required them to drill at least one exploratory well within three years and to surrender 50% of the original licensed area they were granted within four years.

Under the terms the State would gain a "carried interest" by taking a share of the project after a discovery and thus would not have to bear the costs of exploration.

It was clear from the 1975 terms that the Minister envisaged the formation of a State oil company similar to the Norwegian state company, Statoil, if significant finds of oil or gas were made.

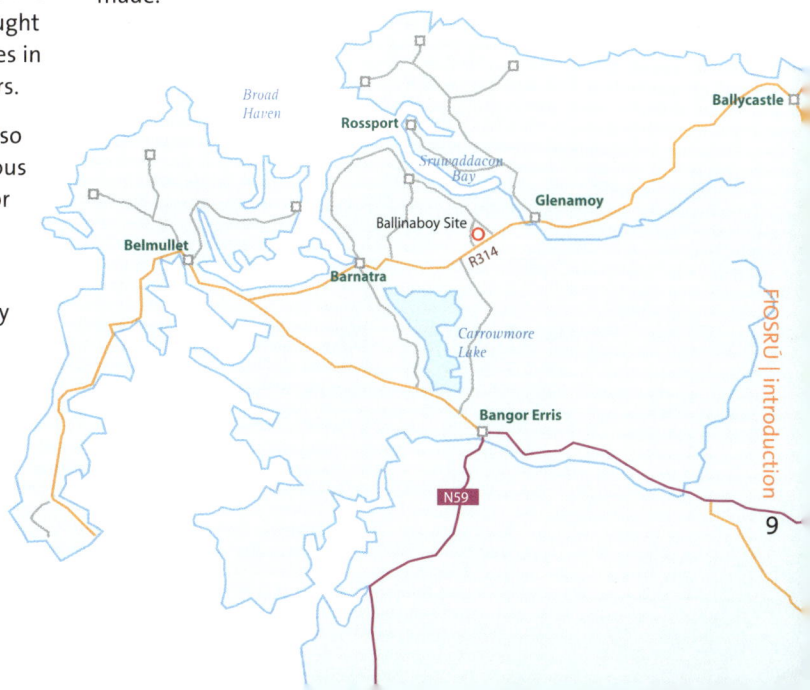

Indeed, as Dáil records examined by the Centre for Public Inquiry (CPI) reveal, the Norwegian government offered direct assistance to their Irish counterparts (partly in exchange for fishing rights in Irish waters) to set up a State oil company and offered them a direct involvement in the commercial development of North Sea fields as a means of gaining the necessary experience and financial ability to properly develop the potentially rich Irish offshore resources.

MINISTER DES O'MALLEY'S ROLE

In 1979, Mr Keating's successor as Minister for Industry and Commerce, Des O'Malley, made a decision to establish the Irish National Petroleum Corporation (INPC), a State company with a remit to control Ireland's strategic petroleum reserves. This initiative, however, was a result of a crisis sparked by the revolution in Iran which disrupted oil supplies and saw a dramatic increase in price. A number of the major oil producing countries would only supply oil to Ireland on condition that it was purchased by a State owned company.

The former Fianna Fáil minister claimed to the Dáil in 2001 that he had been reluctant to establish the INPC and only did so because the government of Iraq would only supply to an Irish state company and Norway's offer to the government of participation in one of its new oil fields was, according to Mr O'Malley, also conditional on the deal being done with an Irish State-controlled company. Despite this radical development the INPC was never given adequate finance or powers to realise its potential and was actually prohibited in its memos and articles of association from drilling for oil and gas.

By the mid 1980s, and despite the drilling of 96 wells offshore, there were no commercial finds of oil or gas and pressure mounted for a dilution of the 1975 fiscal terms.

In April 1985, the then Minister for Energy, Dick Spring, introduced new exploration terms for so-called marginal fields of less than 75 million barrels and announced that he would reduce State royalties and introduce a sliding scale of State participation. In September 1986, he announced the abolition of participation rights for marginal fields.

MINISTER RAY BURKE'S GENEROSITY

In September 1987, Ray Burke, who was given the energy portfolio by Taoiseach, Charles Haughey when the new Fianna Fáil government replaced the Fine Gael–Labour coalition earlier that year,

In September 1987, Ray Burke announced new terms that included the exemption of all oil and gas production from royalty payments and the abolition of all State participation.

announced new terms that included the exemption of all oil and gas production from royalty payments and the abolition of all State participation.

Mr Burke also introduced a 100% tax write-off against profits on capital expenditure for exploration, development and production for up to 25 years. Mr Burke told the Dáil that he thought the removal of the 50% corporation tax rate on profits would be "over generous" and the rate remained. Mr Burke explained that the radical departure from the 1975 terms was necessary in the light of the poor drilling results of previous years and the low price of crude oil.

He said he was gravely concerned that exploration in Irish offshore waters might end if the new regime was not applied. Mr Burke introduced the new terms after several meetings with the executives of a number of oil and gas companies. He also met executives of Marathon Oil to re-negotiate the State's contract for Kinsale gas, on some occasions without the presence of department officials.

MINISTER FOR FINANCE, BERTIE AHERN MAKES HIS MARK

In April 1992, the then Minister for Finance, Bertie Ahern, incorporated Mr Burke's 1987 changes to the taxation regime into the Finance Act and also further reduced corporation tax on oil and gas companies from 50% to 25%.

Mr Ahern told the Dáil that he intended to set out a definitive tax regime that was "designed to improve Ireland's competitive position in attracting oil and gas exploration".

"A particular feature is the provision for a special incentive rate of Corporation tax of 25%, which will apply to income arising under petroleum production leases granted by the Minister for Energy before certain specified dates."

The announcement met with no opposition, with the Labour Party's finance spokesman, Ruairi Quinn, declaring that he would "suspend judgement on the operation of the petroleum taxation regime and the changes being proposed in this Bill because, in fairness, the previous regime did not produce any kind of activity". The Finance Act was passed in late May 1992 while the new licensing terms were introduced with effect from June.

CEDING POWER TO THE OIL COMPANIES

In June 1992, the government introduced new licensing terms with no royalties or state participation. The new licensing terms also permitted producers to sell any oil or gas at market prices – a departure from the arrangement with Marathon Oil, which for many years sold gas from the Kinsale field under a bulk discount supply agreement with Bord Gáis and a radical departure from the 1975 terms.

Critics of the new regime argued that the terms effectively abandoned principles of good offshore management and ceded too much power and rights over the country's natural resources to the oil companies who were now granted 16 year licences for exploration of vast offshore fields.

On 1 January 1993, the British company Enterprise Oil was granted a deepwater licence for six blocks in the Slyne basin. The Enterprise-led consortium also included two Norwegian companies – the State-controlled Statoil and Saga Oil (which, in 1999, sold its 18.5% share to Marathon).

Much of the information about the potential of the Slyne Basin had in fact been collated by officials of the Department of Energy. The Centre for Public Inquiry has learned that significant amounts of the seismic and drilling data collated by the State, particularly from the Slyne and Porcupine Basins, over a period of two decades was made available to the oil companies at a cost of £8000 in respect of at least one report on the Porcupine Basin.

CORRIB IS DISCOVERED A PIPELINE IS PLANNED

In October 1996, Enterprise Oil announced that it had discovered gas in the Corrib Field in the Slyne Basin, 80 kilometres off the Mayo coast, and established a new subsidiary, Enterprise Energy Ireland (EEI), to develop the massive find.

By 1999, the company had identified a site owned by the State forestry service, Coillte, nine kilometres inland at Ballinaboy, County Mayo, for a gas processing plant and started to prepare plans for a pipeline to transport the untreated gas from a wellhead on the seabed.

In the summer of 2000 EEI formally approached Coillte about the purchase of a 400-acre site at Ballinaboy. In July 2000, the Minister for Public Enterprise introduced changes to the Gas (Amendment) Act 2000 that allowed construction of the pipeline by EEI to proceed. Under existing legislative provisions, only Bord Gáis was permitted to construct a gas pipeline.

Broadhaven Bay · Glengad Beach · Rossport Pier

Centre for Public Inquiry

(above) Satellite photograph of Sruwaddacon Bay showing proposed pipeline route and the homes of the Rossport 5 and Bríd McGarry
(credit: John Monaghan)

(below) Panoramic view showing proposed pipeline route from Broadhaven Bay to Ballinaboy Bridge.

In September 2000, the Taoiseach, Bertie Ahern, introduced Statutory Instrument (SI) 110, transferring regulatory power over "any upstream pipeline network" from the Minister for Public Enterprise (who had responsibility for Bord Gáis) to the Minister for the Marine and Natural Resources, Frank Fahey.

In February 2001, Mr Fahey confirmed that he had been informed of the commerciality of the field a month earlier by EEI, which had now applied for a petroleum lease to develop the field.

Significant amounts of the seismic and drilling data collated by the State, particularly from the Slyne and Porcupine Basins, over a period of two decades was made available to the oil companies at a cost of £8000 in respect of at least one report.

Planning permission for the construction of the €800 million processing plant was granted by Mayo County Council in August 2001. The plant, occupying 23 acres, was to be located on the 400-acre site at Ballinaboy Bridge.

The petroleum lease was granted to EEI in November 2001, a day after the minister introduced a further statutory instrument, SI 517, giving him power to make Compulsory Acquisition Orders (CAOs) for upstream pipelines.

This meant that the CAOs made by the minister permitted a private company to occupy land and construct a pipeline even if the owners of the land objected. Within weeks, landowners along the route of the proposed pipeline were informed that they would be served with CAOs unless they accepted compensation and allowed EEI to lay the pipeline.

In March 2002, the Statutory Instruments were incorporated into legislation through an amendment to the Gas Act allowing private companies in the gas market to enter land on the basis of the compulsory acquisition orders made by the Minister. Within weeks of these new measures, giving private companies compulsory acquisition rights that had been previously permitted to local authorities and State or semi-State companies only, Enterprise Oil was taken over by Shell in a €6.5 billion deal.

In April 2002, Mr Fahey approved the EEI plan of development and issued a letter of consent to construct the pipeline; the following month the first CAOs were made by the Minister and provided to EEI.

On the day of the general election on 17 May 2002, Mr Fahey issued a foreshore lease to EEI.

AN BORD PLEANÁLA HEARS THE ARGUMENTS

After objections to the planning permission were filed by Rossport residents and others opposed to the construction of the processing plant, An Bord Pleanála held oral hearings in February and November 2002. Senior planning inspector Kevin Moore heard a range of arguments both in favour of and against the development before coming to his own conclusions.

In his report to An Bord Pleanála Mr Moore stated that the development was on the wrong site. "From a strategic planning perspective this is the wrong site. From the perspective of government policy which seeks to foster regional development, this is the wrong site; from the perspective of minimising environmental impact, this is the wrong site; and consequently, from the perspective of sustainable development, this is the wrong site."

Mr Moore also said that the Marine Licence Vetting Committee, set up in July 2001 to examine the environmental aspects of the Corrib gas field plan of development, the foreshore licence application and the petroleum lease application, had failed to adequately explain why a shallow offshore processing plant, as demanded by many objectors, would not succeed.

The managing director of EEI in Ireland, Andy Pyle, insisted that processing the gas on a shallow-water platform was not economically viable and estimated its cost at €360 million.

Mr Moore recommended refusal of the project on three grounds: the threat to the sensitive and scenic location; the likely instability of the peat bog at Ballinaboy where EEI wished to construct the processing plant; and the risk of a major accident.

AN BORD PLEANÁLA REFUSES PLANNING PERMISSION

At a meeting of An Bord Pleanála in April 2003 the board upheld its inspector's decision but overturned two of the three reasons given by Mr Moore for refusal. It rejected granting planning permission on the grounds that the transfer of 600,000 cubic metres of peat bog to land near the proposed processing plant would represent an unacceptable risk and could pollute local rivers.

While Mr Fahey viewed the An Bord Pleanála decision as a technicality, EEI executives and their senior colleagues at Shell headquarters in London were claiming that the delay in obtaining full planning permission had cost them a further €100 million.

(from left) Former EEI Managing Director Brian Ó Catháin, Principal Officer of the Petroleum Affairs Division Michael Daly and former Minister for the Marine and Natural Resources, Frank Fahey on board drill ship off Donegal, April 2001
(Photo: Shay Fennelly)

BIG OIL MEETS MEETS BIG GOVERNMENT

They sought and were granted a meeting with the Taoiseach, Bertie Ahern, who met with a group of senior Shell executives, including Tom Botts, chief executive officer of Shell E&P Europe, and Andy Pyle of Shell E&P Ireland, in his department on 19 September 2003. Mr Ahern was accompanied by then Minister for Communications, Marine and Natural Resources, Dermot Ahern, and then Minister for Environment, Heritage and Local Government, Martin Cullen.

Assurances were given by Mr Ahern that the government would seek to facilitate the project, which he argued was in the national interest but that it would have to go through the planning process. Assurances were given that any new appeal against planning permission would be addressed swiftly by An Bord Pleanála.

A briefing document prepared for the meeting by the Department of the Environment states that "all possible steps will be taken by the Board to ensure that any such appeal is processed with all possible speed with a view to giving a final decision on it within the statutory objective period of 18 weeks".

Documents obtained under Freedom of Information (FOI) by the Centre for Public Inquiry confirm that the Shell delegation told the Taoiseach that they would like "a greater dialogue with the planning authorities, especially ABP (An Bord Pleanála)".

(from left) Bridie Moran, Barney Keogh, Michael Kane and Ed Collins in the Shell To Sea campaign h.q. in Ballinaboy

OIL INDUSTRY GETS A MEETING WITH AN BORD PLEANÁLA

Within a week a meeting took place between an oil industry delegation, including senior Shell executives, and the chairman of An Bord Pleanála, John O'Connor. According to minutes of the meeting, obtained by the Centre for Public Inquiry, the chairman said that he could not discuss any individual case. The delegation made a presentation titled "The Case for Indigenous Gas" and a discussion took place on the manner in which a large, complex planning application might be approached by a developer.

Shell executive Andy Pyle, Lief Arne Hoyland of Statoil and Fergal Murphy of Marathon Ireland, representing the three elements of the consortium developing the Corrib field, were present along with the chairman of the Irish Offshore Operators Association, Fergus Cahill.

PERMISSION GRANTED DESPITE DANGER SIGNALS

Just hours after the meeting in the Taoiseach's office on 19 September, a massive landslide drove tonnes of peat and mud off Barnacuille and Dooncarton mountains overlooking the route of the pipeline, sweeping away homes and the remains of the deceased in a nearby graveyard. The landslide covered one of the original proposed pipeline routes which, if implemented, would have been carrying unprocessed gas were it not for the planning delays.

In December 2003, EEI submitted a fresh planning application to Mayo County Council, which included a proposal to transfer the 600,000 cubic metres of peat from the Ballinaboy site to a Bord na Móna site 11 kilometres away near Bangor Erris.

In April 2004, the council granted planning permission, which was again appealed to An Bord Pleanála. In October 2004, An Bord Pleanála unanimously approved the planning permission.

Landslide on Barnacuille mountain, 19 September 2003
(Photo: Shay Fennelly)

LOCAL WORRIES

Landowners concerned at the proximity to their homes of the pipeline carrying what they considered untreated and volatile gas, in the shadow of a mountain recently affected by major landslides, continued to protest.

In April 2005, the president of the High Court, Mr Justice Joseph Finnegan, granted an interlocutory injunction to Shell E&P restraining a number of residents from obstructing the laying of the pipeline across their lands.

The residents claimed there was a danger that the pipeline could explode, killing people and damaging houses – some of which were within 70 metres of the pipeline.

Four Courts, Dublin Photo: John Monaghan

THE ASSESSMENT DEBACLE

A Quantitative (Quantified) Risk Assessment (QRA), by UK based pipeline engineering company, J P Kenny, of the risk to human safety caused by the proposed pipeline had argued, in 2001, that the occupants of a building 70 metres away would be safe in the event of a pipeline rupture and explosion. The Erris residents were not convinced and, through local Independent TD Dr Jerry Cowley, sought an independent assessment of the QRA.

In March 2005 the Minister for Communications, Marine and Natural Resources, Noel Dempsey, agreed to commission an independent review of the QRA and this was carried out by the British Pipeline Agency, which largely agreed with the conclusions of the earlier QRA carried out by JP Kenny, whose 2001 report had been commissioned by EEI. Within hours of the review being published in May 2005 it emerged that the British Pipeline Agency was jointly owned by Shell and British Petroleum. This embarrassing disclosure led the Minister, Noel Dempsey, to immediately agree to a fresh review of the QRA.

THE ROSSPORT FIVE BECOME THE NEWS STORY OF THE SUMMER

On 29 June 2005 Micheál Ó Seighin, Willie Corduff, Vincent McGrath, Philip McGrath and Brendan Philbin were sent to Clover Hill jail in Dublin for failing to comply with an order of the High Court restraining them from interfering with Shell E&P's attempts to lay the pipeline.

A major campaign seeking their release made the Rossport Five, as they were soon dubbed, the major news story of the summer. Meetings and rallies took place across the country and the Shell to Sea campaign and the demands of the Erris residents became a national issue.

The demand that Shell process the gas on a shallow platform at sea became the focal point of the growing campaign. The future of the gas processing plant itself was now at stake as residents vowed to stop the pipeline feeding it at any cost.

In July 2005, Minister Dempsey commissioned a third safety review by UK based consultants, Advantica, but the campaigners rejected its terms of reference as too narrow.

The demand that Shell process the gas on a shallow platform at sea became the focal point of the growing campaign. The future of the gas processing plant itself was now at stake as residents vowed to stop the pipeline feeding it at any cost.

Rally in Dublin, the day after the release of the Rossport Five

It also emerged that Shell had breached the consents earlier granted by the minister by constructing sections of the pipeline without permission. Following this further embarrassment which reflected a failure of supervision by the Petroleum Affairs Division (PAD) of his department the Minister established a new Technical Advisory Group to oversee the safety review.

ROSSPORT TO STATOIL AND BACK

On a visit to Statoil headquarters in Norway in September, campaigners for the imprisoned men met senior company executives; they also raised the issue of the five imprisoned men with senior politicians and media representatives during their visit.

Later in September Statoil executives travelled to Ireland for talks with their project partners Shell E&P and Marathon. The Minister, Mr Dempsey, also proposed the appointment of a mediator to try and resolve the impasse between the Rossport 5 and the Shell-led consortium.

On 30 September, Shell moved to have the temporary injunction discharged by the High Court. The Rossport Five were released from jail.

On 12 October, the Department of Communications, Marine and Natural Resources held a two-day public consultation in Geesala, Co. Mayo, chaired by John Gallagher SC, which was sparsely attended. The Rossport Five had rejected

the terms of reference of the safety review, of which the consultation was part, and did not attend.

A report by former Bord Gáis design engineer, Leo Corcoran, was opened at the hearings and raised serious questions about the safety of the proposed pipeline.

On 19 October, the president of the High Court Mr Justice Finnegan said he was satisfied no unauthorised works had been carried out on lands owned by some of the Rossport Five and that there was no breach of an undertaking made to the court by Shell in April. Mr Justice Finnegan said that the issue of unauthorised works by Shell on other lands was a matter between the company and the Minister for the Marine.

On 25 October, the Rossport Five appeared before High Court president Mr Justice Joseph Finnegan in contempt of court proceedings. A decision on further punishment was postponed.

On 28 October, Minister Dempsey rejected the proposal from the Pro Erris Gas Group that Shell pay €250,000 to the local community rather than dismantle a section of the pipeline which had been built without ministerial consent.

On 31 October, the Minister announced that he had appointed Mr Peter Cassells, a former general secretary of the Irish Congress of Trade Unions, to mediate between Shell E&P and the Rossport residents.

A STORM COMES ASHORE

the rossport story

For five years, a few people in the seaside community of Ros Dumhach in northwest Co. Mayo have been fighting to stop an oil consortium led by Shell from building a high-pressure production pipeline carrying untreated gas from the Corrib gas field through their village. When five men refused to allow Shell access to their lands in January 2005, Shell obtained a High Court injunction against the men and the five were locked up for more than three months, drawing national and international attention to their battle against the oil industry.

Micheál Ó Seighin, Willie Corduff, Brendan Philbin, Vincent McGrath and Philip McGrath refused access to their lands because of their concerns about the safety of the pipeline. The five men are residents of Ros Dumhach (known in English as Rossport) in the Gaeltacht area of Kilcommon and have reared families in the area. Philip McGrath is a construction worker and his brother Vincent McGrath, who lives next door, is a musician. Brendan Philbin and Willie Corduff are farmers. All four live along the route of the pipeline, while Micheál Ó Seighin, who lives nearby, is a pensioner who taught the men and many of their neighbours at the local national school.

THE KINSALE MODEL

The Kinsale gas field, discovered and operated by Marathon Oil, has supplied Ireland with natural gas since 1978, creating hundreds of jobs downstream and generating significant revenues for the Exchequer. The Corrib gas field is in a hydrocarbon-rich geological structure on the Atlantic Margin that stretches from the southern coast of Ireland up to the Norwegian continental shelf. The potential value of the Corrib gas lies not only in the availability of supply for Ireland but also in the "downstream" services, which are required to service and process oil and gas. However, under existing exploration and development terms there is no guarantee of supply of gas to the State and no certainty over future price.

When five men refused to allow Shell access to their lands in January 2005, Shell obtained a High Court injunction against the men and the five were locked up for more than three months, drawing national and international attention to their battle against the oil industry.

Willie Corduff on his farm in Gob a' tSáilín

WHAT'S CORRIB WORTH?

An industry presentation to the Irish government in January 1998 estimated the Corrib field and associated nearby fields in the Slyne/Erris basin could contain between 6 and 11 trillion cubic feet (TCF) of natural gas. Natural gas, composed mainly of methane, requires relatively little processing compared to crude oil, which is refined into several products ranging from light oils and petroleum for cars to heavy oils and lubricants. The oil industry measures the value of natural gas by energy equivalence to crude oil, with one trillion cubic feet of natural gas equivalent to between 167 and 182 million barrels of oil. Industry analysts expect oil prices to remain above $50 per barrel in the long term.

It is expected that the price for gas from the Corrib field will be similar to UK "National Balancing Point" prices. Currently, natural gas for immediate (December 2005) delivery is trading at €8.40 per million BTUs (British Thermal Units). At this price, the market value per one trillion cubic feet of Corrib gas is €8.4 billion, putting the potential value of the Corrib and surrounding fields for Shell and its partners in excess of €50.4 billion.

The Rossport Five, who were initially concerned about the safety of the pipeline and the apparent abdication by the State of its constitutional obligation to protect and defend the rights of its citizens, are now demanding a re-negotiation of the 1992 licensing terms and fiscal regime under which the Corrib gas field and Ireland's other offshore oil and gas resources are being developed.

The market value per one trillion cubic feet of Corrib gas is €8.4 billion, putting the potential value of the Corrib and surrounding fields for Shell and its partners in excess of €50.4 billion.

GAS IS DISCOVERED OFF ERRIS

In 1996, Enterprise Oil announced the discovery of a gas field 80 kilometres off the Mayo coast. Enterprise, with a 45% share in the project, was the operator in a consortium with Saga Petroleum (which sold its 18.5% share to Marathon in 1999) and Statoil (36.5%). Enterprise drilled appraisal wells in 1998 and 1999 and declared the field commercial in early 2001.

WHERE TO BRING IT ASHORE?

In 1998, the Corrib Enterprise Oil consortium employed consultants to survey the Connacht coastline for suitable landfall locations to bring the gas ashore. The consultants identified locations at Killala Bay, Broadhaven Bay and Blacksod Bay, Emlagh Point (west of Westport) and Liscannor Bay and Doughmore Bay in Co. Clare. Unprocessed gas from undersea fields can only be piped a certain distance, which limited the site selection to Killala Bay and Broadhaven Bay. The developer identified four sites within these areas – Sruwaddacon Bay, Bunatrahir Bay, Ross Point close to Killala, and Rathlee Head – but dismissed the Killala Bay option because of the 145-kilometre distance. Bunatrahir and Rathlee Head were dismissed because of the visual intrusion that a coast-based terminal would present. That left Broadhaven Bay, 80 kilometres from the field, as the preferred location.

A LAND-BASED TERMINAL

The developers also needed a gas processing facility and a site was identified at Ballinaboy Bridge as a suitable location. In the summer of 1999, state forestry agency Coillte moved to bring the 400-acre forestry site into its legal title. In March 2000, Enterprise Energy Ireland (EEI), the Irish subsidiary of Enterprise Oil, engaged RSK Environment Limited to prepare an Environmental Impact Statement (EIS) on the Ballinaboy site. EEI formally approached Coillte to purchase the site in May 2000.

The availability of the Coillte site, which EEI purchased in 2001 for a sum in excess of €2.7 million, accommodated EEI's development concept of a land-based terminal. In his 2003 report on the planning appeal over the processing plant site, An Bord Pleanála's Senior Planning Inspector Kevin Moore wrote: "A conclusion can reasonably be made from the information before the Board that the chosen development concept for the Corrib Gas Field by its nature led to the selection of a large land-based terminal site. The availability of a

large land-based site in one ownership with the land area to accommodate a processing terminal at Ballinaboy greatly accommodated the development concept for the Corrib Field."

FROM EXCITEMENT TO FOREBODING

This decision to base the terminal at Ballinaboy was made before the local community knew about the project. People first heard of the development in Spring 2000, when local fishermen said they had been paid £2,000 apiece by EEI to stay away from the area of the rig and the inshore development. During the summer of 2000, EEI began to seek support for their plans among the Erris community and donated £8,000 to Carne Golf Club. The Bishop of Killala, Tom Finnegan, and Kilcommon parish priest Fr Declan Caulfield were flown out to bless the rig.

Initially, locals were excited about the prospect. "We thought we would have gas coming into Co. Mayo," said Annie Gannon, who owns land and commonage along the planned pipeline route. "Our son was working up in Dublin at the time,

People first heard of the development in spring 2000, when local fishermen said they had been paid £2,000 apiece by EEI to stay away from the area of the rig and the inshore development. During the summer of 2000, EEI began to seek support for their plans among the Erris community and donated £8,000 to Carne Golf Club.

and he and other people thought that they would have jobs to come back to." Construction of the pipeline and the gas processing plant promised the creation of up to 500 local jobs in an area with an unemployment rate of more than 30%. At that point residents assumed the pipeline was to carry clean gas but soon learned the distinction between an upstream and a downstream pipeline. The upstream pipeline will carry unprocessed gas, which contains a volatile mix of chemical compounds, from the subsea field to the gas processing plant while the downstream pipeline carries clean, processed and consumer ready gas.

HERITAGE, BEAUTY, HISTORY AND NEGLECT

The barony of Erris has suffered centuries of neglect and mismanagement. In the second half of the 19th century, there was massive emigration from the area to Britain and the United States. The principal source of income in late 19th-century Erris was money from relatives abroad, a flow of remittances which continued, like mass emigration, into the 1960s.

Two thousand people live in Kilcommon, which contains one of the few Gaeltacht areas remaining in Ireland. The economy depends on small-scale farming and seasonal fishing, and the area has consistently suffered from emigration because of a lack of local jobs. The nearest towns are Bangor-Erris and Belmullet.

Rossport is in the parish of Kilcommon, which lies between Belmullet and Ballycastle along the north coast road in Co. Mayo. Along the coast, the sea has carved spectacular cliffs that rise to more than 300 metres. The Blue Stack Mountains rise to the north, and Benbulben and Knocknarea rise to the east. This region, with its megalithic tombs and stone circles, is one of the oldest inhabited areas of the world. The world heritage site at the Céide Fields along the coast road celebrates a prehistoric landscape that contains the world's oldest known field systems, the early agricultural endeavours of five thousand years ago.

It is an unpolluted, sensitive and scenic landscape. The air is clean, and much of the local population draws its drinking water from Carrowmore Lake. Several locations around Sruwaddacon Bay and the planned processing plant site are designated or proposed protection areas. The proposed landfall site for the pipeline at Glengad beach at Broadhaven Bay is a proposed candidate Special Area of Conservation (SAC) and a designated Area of Special Scenic Importance. The Glenamoy Bog Complex including Sruwaddacon Bay is an SAC, as is Carrowmore Lake. Pollatomish Bog is an SAC and a proposed Natural Heritage Area.

Along the coast, the sea has carved spectacular cliffs that rise to more than 300 metres. The Blue Stack Mountains rise to the north, and Benbulben and Knocknarea rise to the east. This region, with its megalithic tombs and stone circles, is one of the oldest inhabited areas of the world. The world heritage site at the Céide Fields along the coast road celebrates a prehistoric landscape that contains the world's oldest known field systems

AN IMPORTANT MARINE HABITAT

In 2001, Enterprise Energy Ireland Ltd commissioned a report from the Coastal and Marine Resources Centre at University College Cork titled "Marine mammal monitoring in the waters of Broadhaven Bay & northwest Mayo: 2001–2002". The authors of the report cited over 220 sightings of two whale and five dolphin and otter species during 2002. The report stated: "Broadhaven Bay SAC and its neighbouring coastal waters undoubtedly represent an important area for marine mammals and other species. There are few, if any, comparable examples of a relatively small, discrete bay in Ireland containing all five Annex II marine mammal species [Bottlenose dolphin, harbour porpoise, grey seal, common seal and European otter] with such frequency. It was also clear in 2001–2002 that the area contained important foraging habitats for numerous marine mammal species, plankton-feeding basking sharks and seabirds. Recurrent encounters with photo-identifiable bottlenose dolphins during 2002 and sightings of newborn common and white-sided dolphin calves also underlined the area's potential as a breeding/rearing habitat for several cetacean species."

According to the Environmental Impact Statement submitted to Mayo County Council in support of the EEI planning application, there was "no evidence that the bay is of particular importance" to whales and dolphins.

The two men most closely associated with the project during the critical legislative changes between 2000 and 2002 were Taoiseach, Bertie Ahern and the Galway West TD and Minister for the Marine and Natural Resources, Frank Fahey

An Taoiseach Bertie Ahern

Photocall Ireland

Frank Fahey (Former Minister for the Marine and Natural Resources)

GOVERNMENT OILS THE WHEELS OF LEGISLATION

The approach by Enterprise Energy Ireland in 2000 to purchase the 400-acre Coillte site at Ballinaboy Bridge, nine kilometres inland from Broadhaven Bay, created significant legislative problems for the Government and the Department of the Marine and Natural Resources, as existing legislation did not cover an on-land, upstream pipeline network.

The pipeline would have to run through private property, but there was no legislation to allow the Minister to make compulsory acquisition orders (CAOs) and provide them to private corporations. The Government placed the project under the supervision of the Department of the Marine and Natural Resources, which controlled fisheries, forestry and Bord na Móna, in addition to oil and gas exploration and production, and the department took responsibility for both planning and health and safety aspects of the Corrib project.

The two men most closely associated with the project during the critical legislative changes between 2000 and 2002 were Taoiseach, Bertie Ahern and the Galway West TD and Minister for

Bertie Ahern, announced that Bord Gáis and the EEI consortium would fund and build a connector pipeline from the Ballinaboy site to the national loop at Galway. The announcement was made before any application for planning permission for the project was submitted

Brendan Philbin with his daughter Siobhán and wife Aggie

the Marine and Natural Resources, Frank Fahey. On 10 July 2000, the Government introduced the first stages of a complex series of legislative acts designed to place the gas pipeline outside the domain of planning through the Gas (Amendment) Act of 2000, which made provision for "a person other than the Board (i.e. Bord Gáis)" to construct or operate a pipeline and cleared the way for EEI to apply for planning permission for the processing plant.

In September 2000, Mr Ahern introduced Statutory Instrument (SI) 110 of 2000, transferring regulatory power over "any upstream pipeline network" from the Minister for Public Enterprise (who had responsibility for Bord Gáis) to the Minister for the Marine and Natural Resources.

In early October 2000, at a 21st anniversary celebration of Bord Gáis, An Taoiseach, Bertie Ahern, announced that Bord Gáis and the EEI consortium would fund and build a connector pipeline from the Ballinaboy site to the national loop at Galway. The announcement was made before any application for planning permission for the project was submitted by the developers.

EIS SETS OFF ALARM BELLS

In November 2000, EEI applied for planning permission to Mayo County Council and submitted an Environmental Impact Statement (EIS). Rossport resident, Gerard Muller, and local geography teacher, Micheál Ó Seighin, went to the Garda station in Belmullet to inspect the EIS. They were shocked by what they saw. The EIS indicated that gas would come ashore at high pressure in a raw state, containing metals and radioactive gas.

The EIS indicated that gas would come ashore at high pressure in a raw state, containing metals and radioactive gas.

"The proposal to redistribute 60 acres of peat (10 to 15 ft. deep) within the local forestry area seems to have come out of the teddy bears' picnic"

Mr Ó Seighin drafted a submission to Mayo County Council outlining the objections of local residents. "The entire community here now realises the scale and toxicity of the effluents and emissions about to be imposed on this area – land, air and sea – by the construction and refining activities of Corrib Gas," he wrote. Mr Ó Séighin zeroed in on the proposals to excavate large amounts of peat to make way for the processing plant: "The proposal to redistribute 60 acres of peat (10 to 15 ft. deep) within the local forestry area seems to have come out of the teddy bears' picnic. Apart from the sheer bulk and viscosity of the mass, the logistics rival those of NATO in Kosovo. Enterprise Oil have not in any way shown (a) that they understand the problem and (b) that they have any idea how to cope with it." The council requested further details and the developer re-submitted the planning application along with a more detailed EIS.

Early in 2001, EEI applied to the Department of the Marine and Natural Resources for a petroleum lease for the Corrib field. On 15 February 2001, Minister Fahey told the Dáil that the consortium had notified him of the commerciality of the field on 11 January 2001.

THE INDEPENDENT CONSULTANTS

In December of 2000, the Department of the Marine and Natural Resources had asked Enterprise Energy Ireland for a study of alternatives to the onshore processing plant, which the company submitted in January 2001. The department forwarded the report to their consultant petroleum engineer, David Fox, who operates a UK-based petroleum consultancy, David Fox and Associates, specialising in developing low-cost tie-backs (where a subsea well-head is tied back to a processing plant on an offshore platform or on land) for oil and gas production. Speaking in the Dáil on 8 February 2005, Minister for Communications, Marine and Natural Resources, Noel Dempsey, said: "In December 2000, my Department requested from the developers the results of its alternative concept studies. These were examined and reviewed in January 2001 by the consultant petroleum engineer advising my Department. He advised the Department that the developers of the Corrib gas field should not be required to change or consider changing the Corrib development scheme."

Former school teachers Micheál Ó Seighin and his wife Caitlín

Rossport residents told Mike Daly of the Petroleum Affairs Division (PAD) that the Minister could not grant CAOs for the upstream pipeline to private corporations. Later that month, Taoiseach Bertie Ahern introduced SI 389 of 2001, transferring powers from the Minister for Public Enterprise to the Minister for the Marine and Natural Resources covering all legislation relating to upstream pipeline networks.

THE MARINE LICENCE VETTING COMMITTEE

In July 2001, the department convened the Marine Licence Vetting Committee (MLVC) to examine the environmental aspects of the Corrib gas field plan of development, foreshore licence application and petroleum lease application, with terms of reference covering the entire pipeline and the processing plant.

The committee comprised Dr Terry McMahon and Dr Francis O'Beirn of the Marine Institute, Trevor Champ from the Central Fisheries Board and three officials from the Department of the Marine and Natural Resources: Mick O'Driscoll, Richard McKeever and Captain Tom O'Callaghan. The committee and the department hired in outside consultants, with the MLVC retaining consultants Posford Haskoning, a subsidiary of engineering and architectural consultants Royal Haskoning. The department retained international consultants Environmental Resources Management (ERM).

On 25 July 2001, chief geologist Dr Keith Robinson and Mike Daly of the Petroleum Affairs Division (PAD) of the Department of the Marine and Natural Resources, and Minister Frank Fahey, travelled to Geesala, Co. Mayo, to host a public consultation on the project. Rossport residents told Daly that the Minister could not grant CAOs for the upstream pipeline to private corporations. Later that month, Taoiseach Bertie Ahern introduced SI 389 of 2001, transferring powers from the Minister for Public Enterprise to the Minister for the Marine and Natural Resources covering all legislation relating to upstream pipeline networks.

Mayo County Council granted planning permission on 3 August 2001, and Rossport residents appealed the decision to An Bord Pleanála.

The government moved to provide the land for the pipeline by giving powers to the Minister to make Compulsory Acquisition Orders for the benefit of a private consortium. Rather than altering existing legislation on CAOs, which were granted through the Minister for Public Enterprise, the government moved part of the CAO legislation into the power of the Department of the Marine and Natural Resources, without the caveats relating to the public interest.

POWER MOVES QUICKLY

On 15 November 2001, Mr Fahey introduced SI 517 of 2001, giving the Minister for the Marine and Natural Resources powers to grant CAOs for upstream pipelines.

On 16 November 2001, Mr Fahey granted the petroleum lease to EEI at a cost of €3 million.

On 21 November, Enterprise Energy Ireland applied to the Department for approval of its plan of development, foreshore licence and consent to build the pipeline, and submitted a new Environmental Impact Statement.

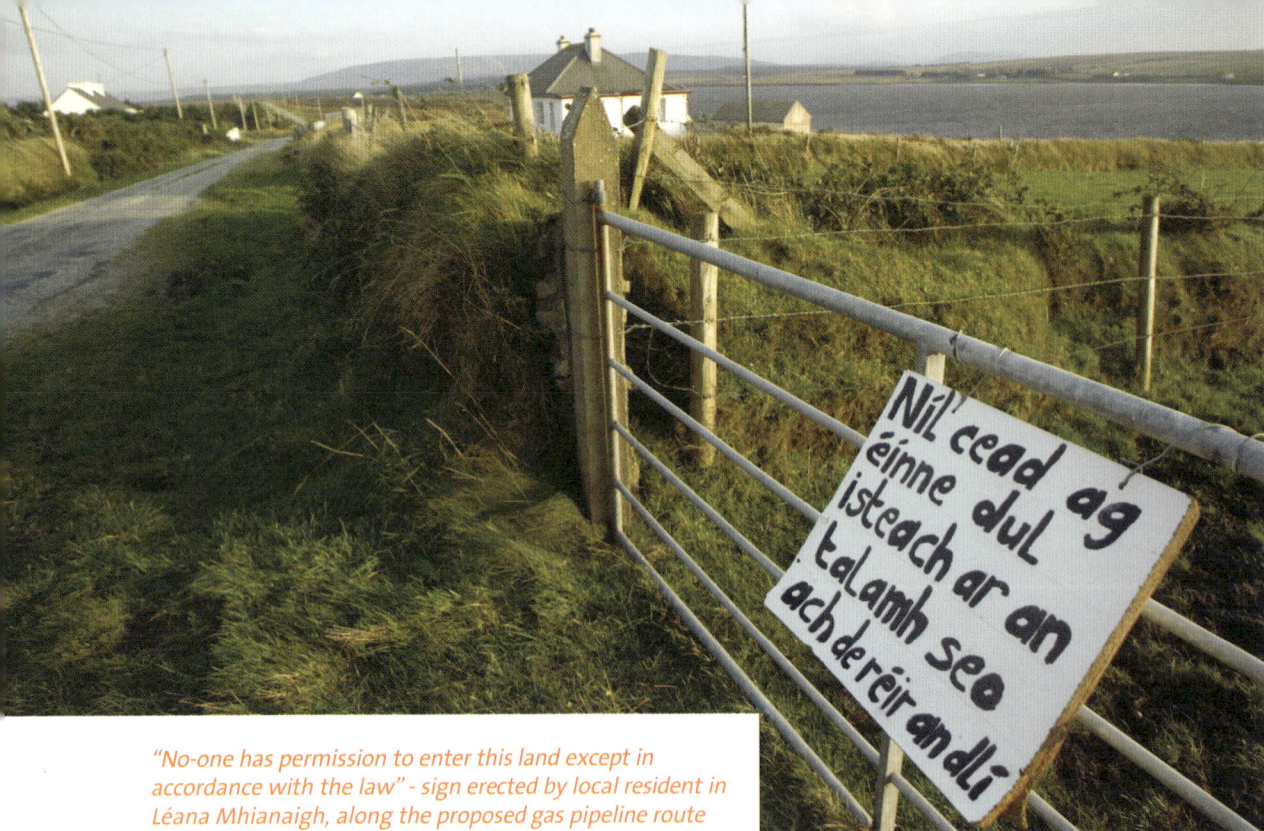

"No-one has permission to enter this land except in accordance with the law" - sign erected by local resident in Léana Mhianaigh, along the proposed gas pipeline route

BIG OIL GOES DOOR TO DOOR

On 17 December 2001, Enterprise Energy Ireland representatives began knocking on doors and sending letters to landowners asking them to grant permission for the pipeline in exchange for compensation. Twenty-seven people held shares in the commonage, and seven people owned land along the route of the pipeline. EEI told landowners that they would be served with CAOs unless they signed up to the compensation offer. Those who owned parts of the commonage but did not live adjacent to the route of the pipeline signed, but seven of the landowners refused. Concerned about the safety of the pipeline and the potential danger to their families, they refused to sign until they received guarantees about the pipeline's safety.

In February 2002, An Bord Pleanála Senior Planning Inspector, Kevin Moore, opened the oral hearing in Ballina, County Mayo, to hear appeals against planning permission. The first hearing convened for two weeks and was then adjourned.

THE VETTING COMMITTEE APPROVES DEVELOPMENT

The Vetting Committee (MLVC) report, published in April 2002, approved the development with 28 conditions. Opponents of the project had become convinced that the safest option was to process the gas offshore on a shallow-water platform, and several of the submissions to the MLVC raised the issue of offshore processing. However, the Vetting Committee report dismissed the alternative option:

> *"Treatment of gas at source requires manned platforms or vessels. The MLVC has considered these methodologies and has noted that the coastline of the west of Ireland is exposed to a vigorous wave climate characterized by one of the highest wave power levels in the world (Ireland's Marine and Coastal Areas and Adjacent Seas: An Environmental Assessment 1999). Given the water depths and the extremely hostile nature of the environment in this part of the Atlantic, the MLVC is of the opinion that there would be greater environmental risk and risk to human life through treating it at source. The MLVC accordingly recommends onshore treatment of gas".*

The Vetting Committee, however, only considered treatment at source – 80 kilometres out to sea – and failed to consider a shallow-water platform near shore for processing, but with the Vetting Committee report in place, the department began to issue the approvals for the plan of development, the pipeline consents and the foreshore licence.

PUSHING THROUGH LEGISLATION BEFORE THE 2002 GENERAL ELECTION

In the Spring of 2002, the government began another series of legislative changes to assist the project. The Department of the Marine and Natural Resources hired UK-based petroleum consultant Andrew Johnston to carry out a review of the design code for the pipeline. Mr Johnston submitted his review on 13 February 2002 and recommended minor changes to the Quantitative (Quantified) Risk Assessment (QRA).

A QRA is a mathematical modelling tool used by engineers to quantify risk to human safety, and the Government reviews of the QRA have proved to be one of the most contentious aspects of the project. The first QRA, which was produced in November 2001 by JP Kenny, has not been released, and five further versions have been prepared since the initial assessment. On the basis of Mr Johnston's report, the department moved to issue consents for the pipeline.

On 27 March 2002, Minister for State at the Department of Public Enterprise Joe Jacob moved to amend the 1976 Gas Act and told the Seanad that the amendment "would ensure that Bord Gáis Éireann and all other operators in the gas market have exactly the same rights under the Gas Act, 1976, in regard to entry into land and the making of compulsory acquisition orders". The Dáil passed the Gas (Interim) (Regulation) Act 2002 on 10 April 2002, allowing Enterprise Energy Ireland (EEI) to apply for privileges that had only previously been granted to local authorities and State or semi-State bodies. Within weeks, Enterprise Oil was taken over by Shell.

Enterprise Oil had been a takeover target for several years. In early 2002, the Italian company ENI had expressed interest in a bid, but British Energy Minister Brian Wilson announced that he wanted Enterprise to stay under British control. Within one week of the Gas Act amendment, Shell made a €6.5 billion bid for Enterprise Oil, and on 2 April 2002 the board of Enterprise Oil decided to accept the offer.

> "Ahern told me he knew we weren't just a NIMBY (Not In My Back Yard) group, but that the project was in the national interest, and that it was going to go through."

FRANK FAHEY APPROVES PLAN

On 15 April 2002, following the recommendations of the MLVC, Mr Fahey approved the EEI plan of development and issued a letter of consent to construct the pipeline. In his letter of consent the Minister specified that the pipeline should be a minimum distance of 70 metres from dwellings. The letter did not specify under which code of practice the pipeline should be constructed. On 3 May, the Minister made the first of the CAOs and provided them to EEI.

When Taoiseach, Bertie Ahern, visited Geesala in Mayo shortly before the May 2002 general election, a delegation representing the residents approached him. Micheál Ó Seighin spoke for the residents. "I argued that there were other ways to do the project, and asked him to give me his economic people for a couple of hours," said Ó Seighin. "Ahern told me he knew we weren't just a NIMBY (Not In My Back Yard) group, but that the project was in the national interest, and that it was going to go through."

MR FAHEY ISSUES LEASE ON DAY OF GENERAL ELECTION

On 17 May, Frank Fahey issued the foreshore lease to EEI. It was the day of the general election. The Fianna Fáil-led coalition was re-elected and Mr Fahey was appointed as Minister of State at the Department of Enterprise, Trade and Employment with responsibility for Labour Affairs in the new Fianna Fáil–Progressive Democrat cabinet.

An Bórd Pleanála hearings, February 2002 in Ballina
(Photo: Shay Fennelly)

THE BORD PLEANÁLA HEARINGS

In July 2002, Bord Pleanála requested further information from the Corrib developer. Hearings re-commenced in November 2002 and finished on 10 December. In April 2003, An Bord Pleanála published its decision to refuse planning permission.

SENIOR PLANNING INSPECTOR VIGOROUSLY OPPOSES PLAN

In his report, Senior Planning Inspector Kevin Moore was adamant that the development was taking place on the wrong site:

"From a strategic planning perspective, this is the wrong site; from the perspective of Government policy which seeks to foster balanced regional development, this is the wrong site; from the perspective of minimising environmental impact, this is the wrong site; and consequently, from the perspective of sustainable development, this is the wrong site.

At a time when the Board in now required, in accordance with the Local Government (Planning and Development) Act, 2000, to have regard to the proper planning and **sustainable** *development of an area in which a development is proposed to be constructed, it is my submission that the proposed development of a large gas processing terminal at this rural, scenic, and unserviced area on a bogland hill some 8 kilometres inland from the Mayo coastland landfall location, with all its site development works difficulties, public safety concerns, adverse visual, ecological, and traffic impacts, and a range of other significant environmental impacts, defies any rational understanding of the term "sustainability". It is an irony that this large industrial proposal is linked with a natural gas resource, the exploitation of which adheres to the concept of sustainability."*

Mr Moore noted that several separate agencies had responsibility for the development for seabed, landfall, overland pipes and terminal:

"If there is to be any merit in permitting the splitting of this overall project into its various component parts and permitting separate independent assessments by various agencies, then the Board should not be constrained by any decisions that may or may not have been made by other agencies to date, in my opinion."

MR MOORE SCATHING ABOUT MLVC REPORT

Mr Moore was scathing about the MLVC report:

"How the MLVC came to its conclusions would appear to be beyond the realms of a rational approach to the planning of this major infrastructural development and exhibits nothing short of prematurity, in my view, when the decision of the Board on the critical issue of where best to locate a terminal had not been made in April, 2002. Their determinations should not be utilised as a stick for driving the Board in the direction of a grant of planning permission in this way. Their deliberations are not the determinants on whether this development should be granted planning permission or not. In effect, if this was to be the case, the Board's function has been undermined in determining the proper planning and sustainable development of this area."

Shell To Sea campaigner and teacher Maura Harrington at a community meeting in Glenamoy, October 2005

> "From a strategic planning perspective this is the wrong site; from the perspective of government policy which seeks to foster regional development, this is the wrong site; from the perspective of minimising environmental impact, this is the wrong site; and from the perspective of sustainable development, this is the wrong site."

Aerial view of the site of the proposed Gas Processing Plant in Ballinaboy looking south west, with Carrowmore Lake in the background (Photo: Jan Pesch)

DEVELOPER DID NOT ADDRESS QUESTIONS

Mr Moore noted the MLVC's approval of the plan of development emphasised "a perception to some degree that the granting of planning permission for the processing terminal at the Ballinaboy site is a *fait accompli*".

Mr Moore also noted that the MLVC report compared the treatment of gas at source versus onshore:

> "It did not compare the treatment of gas onshore with a shallow water option, i.e. offshore but not at source. The utilisation of the findings of the MLVC are not appropriate in this instance when considering what was asked of the applicant by way of further information. Furthermore, the applicant appears to be seeking to use the findings of the MLVC to undermine the deliberations of the Board on the suitability of the Ballinaboy site from a planning perspective."

Mr Moore had investigated the shallow-water option that the MLVC had failed to consider and he had requested the developer to provide further information on the tie-backs in the re-opened hearings. David Bennett of Granherne, an oil and gas development solutions company owned by US company, Halliburton, submitted on behalf of the developer that the Broadhaven Bay option was the limit of current technology and, therefore, the only acceptable option. Mr Moore noted that the response provided by Granherne did not address the questions he had raised. "It was expressly requested that a more complete comparison be made between the proposed development and a shallow water fixed steel jacket option," Mr Moore wrote. "The applicant's response completely avoided this option."

Mr Moore's analysis of the Granherne submission showed that the developments submitted as evidence of comparable existing subsea tie-backs were all tied back to offshore platforms. Several of these fields, including the Gemini field, Mica field

Independent TD, Jerry Cowley at a community meeting in Glenamoy, October 2005

FIOSRÚ | the rossport story

35

Philip McGrath on his land in Rossport

and Pluto fields in the Gulf of Mexico, were smaller than the Corrib field. "Canyon Express [in the Gulf of Mexico] is a gas field that has a comparable reserve," Mr Moore wrote.

"Again, it is tied back to a shallow water platform, a distance of 88km, and the processing platform stands in a water depth of 91m. This is a new processing platform. Its umbilical is in two sections. For comparative purposes, it is a reasonable example in my opinion. The applicant has sought to minimise the comparison by submitting that a platform was viable as a consequence of the presence of an existing pipeline, because of the relatively benign physical environment, and due to other hydrocarbon prospectivity in the area."

(The destructive potential of hurricanes in the Gulf of Mexico illustrated starkly by Hurricane Katrina which destroyed much of New Orleans in September 2005 was clearly understated in the submissions to the inspector.)

MOORE DISMISSES COMPARISONS

Mr Moore noted that the norm appeared to be tie-backs to offshore platforms. He dismissed the comparison with the planned developments at Ormen Lange and Snohvit on the Norwegian coastline, which were to process vast fields several times the size of the Corrib gas field.

However, the issue of Ormen Lange and Snohvit raised further questions. The oil industry had told the Government in January 1998 that the offshore

around the Corrib field potentially contained up to 11 TCF (or eleven times the size of the Corrib field). In his report, Mr Moore wrote about the prospect of further gas being discovered in the area: "I put it to the Board that there is hydrocarbon prospectivity ongoing off the coast of Donegal, that the proposed gas terminal has a design life of 30 years, and that it was accepted at the hearing that the terminal could be developed to meet new demands from other prospectivity if a tie-back was feasible."

Andy Pyle, Managing Director of Enterprise Energy Ireland, had submitted that the Corrib field was only viable as a subsea tie-back and said that the shallow-water platform was not economically viable. Mr Pyle estimated the cost of an offshore platform at €360 million and a 40% increase in annual operating costs.

Maureen and Vincent McGrath standing 20 metres from proposed pipeline route, opposite the entrance to their home.

NATIONAL STRATEGIC IMPORTANCE OF TERMINAL QUESTIONED

Mr Moore stressed that the development of the gas processing terminal was not of national strategic importance. "This is a critical point," he wrote.

> "The planned developments for the improvement of gas infrastructure in Ireland are in place or are currently being put in place by Bord Gáis. The proposed development under appeal allows a reserve to be exploited that would feed an estimated 60% of the resource into the national network and out of the West and North-West Regions. The lack of any benefits to these regions (outside of Galway) is compounded by the wholly inappropriate site proposed to be developed. There is no merit in permitting this large industrial development on the wrong site. It is critically important to apply the best development concept and to seek out a terminal site that minimises such adverse environmental impacts that would arise with the current development proposal. In my opinion, the current proposed site is unequivocally an incorrect choice."

MR MOORE RECOMMENDS REFUSAL

In his concluding remarks, Mr Moore recommended refusal of the project on three grounds, specifically the threat to the sensitive and scenic location; the likely instability of the

"The lack of any benefits to these regions (outside of Galway) is compounded by the wholly inappropriate site proposed to be developed. There is no merit in permitting this large industrial development on the wrong site."

peat; and the risk of a major accident. Mr Moore wrote: "The Board is not satisfied, having regard to the significant adverse environmental effects of the proposed development, that the development at Ballinaboy constitutes the optimum solution to providing a gas processing terminal to serve the Corrib Gas Field." Mr Moore noted the possible instability of the peat that was to be moved to the perimeter of the Ballinaboy site:

> "The Board is not satisfied that the site development works can be undertaken without undermining the safety of road users and causing structural damage to the adjoining Regional Road R314 and to adjoining properties. The proposed development would, therefore, endanger the health and safety of the general public in the vicinity of the site, seriously injure the amenities of property in the vicinity, and adversely affect the use of the regional road."

Mr Moore noted that the developer had not satisfied the provisions for safety under the EU "Seveso II" directive on the transport of dangerous materials. He wrote that the Board was not satisfied that "the proposed development would not give rise to an unacceptable risk to members of the public due to the proximity of the terminal site to residential properties and areas of public use to which the Directive applies".

(Mr Moore's inquiry extended only to the gas processing plant and excluded consideration of safety issues associated with the proposed pipeline as it is exempt from normal planning procedures. The Inspector did not take into account the dangers posed by landslides in the area as these occurred after the completion of his report.)

AN BORD PLEANÁLA REFUSES PERMISSION

Following a meeting of An Bord Pleanála on 28 and 29 April 2003, the Board directed that planning permission be refused, but overturned two of the three reasons Mr Moore gave for refusal – the visual impact on a sensitive landscape and failure to comply with the Seveso directive on dangerous substances – and rejected planning solely on the grounds that the transfer of 600,000 cubic metres of peat bog would present an unacceptable risk and could pollute the local rivers. Minister of State for Labour Affairs, Frank Fahey, announced that the project had been delayed on a "technicality".

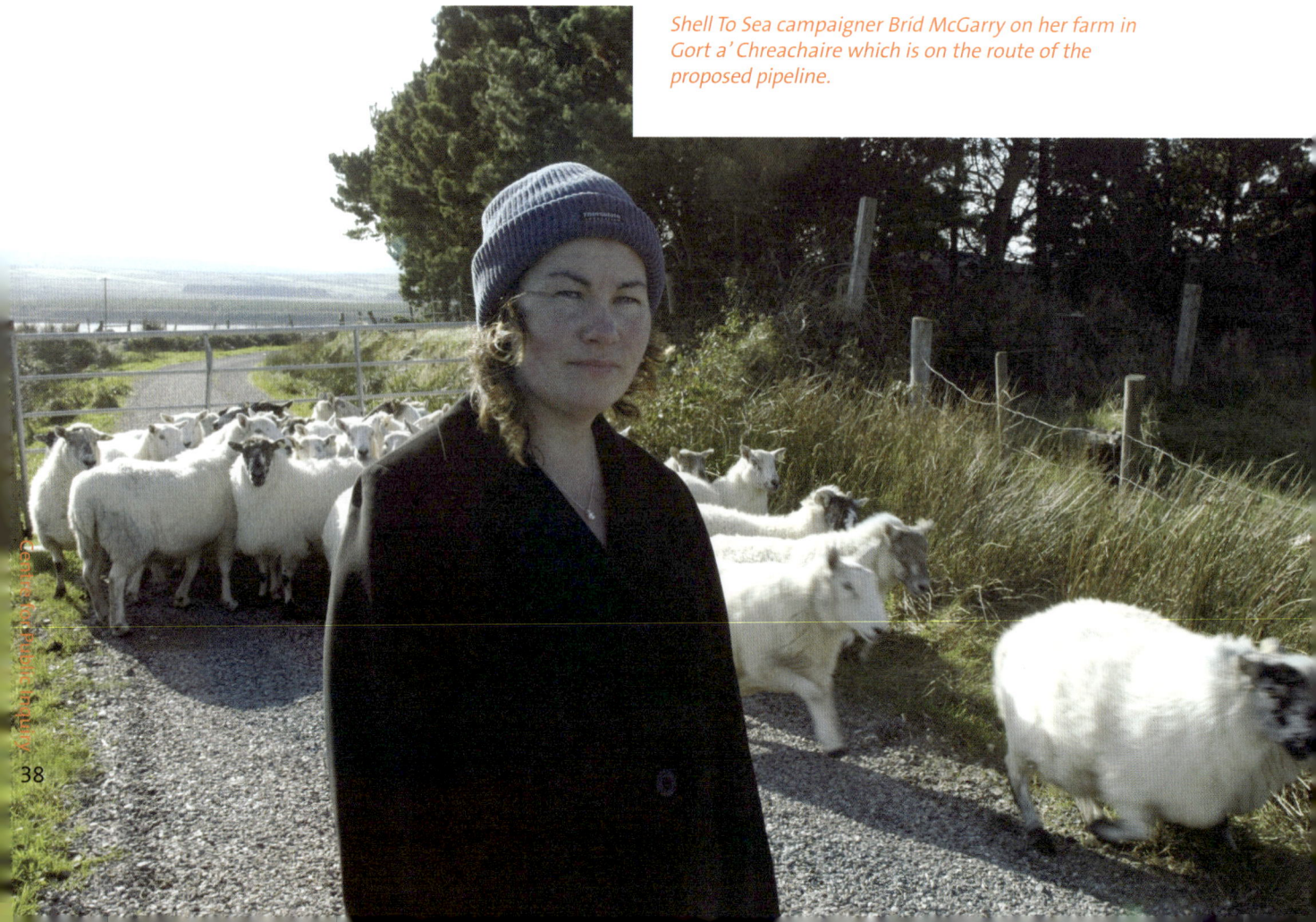

Shell To Sea campaigner Bríd McGarry on her farm in Gort a' Chreachaire which is on the route of the proposed pipeline.

Andy Pyle, Managing Director, Shell E&P Ireland Ltd.
(Photo: Shay Fennelly)

"An Bord Pleanála has recently given the Government an assurance that should an appeal be made to the Board against a planning authority decision relating to development of the Corrib gas field it will be afforded top priority by the Board as an item of national infrastructure."

BIG OIL COURTS BIG GOVERNMENT

On August 6 2003, the chief executive officer of Shell E&P, Mr Walter van de Vijver, wrote to the Taoiseach requesting a meeting about the project. Mr Ahern agreed to the meeting.

Under Freedom of Information legislation, the CPI obtained briefing documents prepared for the meeting by the Department of the Environment, Heritage and Local Government and the Department of Communications, Marine and Natural Resources.

Briefing documents for the meeting held on 19 September, 2003, from the Department of the Environment, Heritage and Local Government state: "An Bord Pleanála has recently given the Government an assurance that should an appeal be made to the Board against a planning authority decision relating to development of the Corrib gas field it will be afforded top priority by the Board as an item of national infrastructure."

The document dated 12 September 2003 and prepared for the 19 September meeting by the Department of Environment officials continued: "Consequently all possible steps will be taken by the Board to ensure that any such appeal is processed with all possible speed with a view to giving a final decision on it within the statutory period of 18 weeks."

According to briefing documents prepared for the same meeting by the Department of Communications, Marine and Natural Resources:

"EEIL are very concerned with the following:

The length of time (20 months) for ABP's [An Bord Pleanála] to arrive at its decision; ABPs lack of understanding of many aspects of both the project and the petroleum sector as exhibited in the Inspector's report;

The disimprovement in the economics of the project (this also impacts on the potential corporation tax yield to the State) resulting from the delay in the ABP planning process;

The need for ABP to engage directly with the developers of what can be termed national and strategic infrastructure projects.

EEIL continues to have serious reservations as to their understanding of the ABP decision and especially the final sentence which states 'the Board noted that alternatives are available for the development of the Corrib Gas Field'.

The image on the left shows a table-shaped sign attached to the rear of a car reading:

> **Who Benefits**
> Norway (statoil)   36.5%
> SHELL   45%
> Marathon   18.5%
> Politicians   ???↑%
> IRELAND   0%

The document concluded that EEIL were engaged in a full review of the project and were considering, among other options, relocating the terminal to 'Ballinacorrick' (*sic* – presumably Bellacorick) or the former Asahi site in County Mayo. The document also states that an offshore processing platform was under consideration but adds, "this is not viewed as a viable option".

MR AHERN MEETS THE OIL INDUSTRY

On the morning of 19 September 2003, Mr Ahern met with Tom Botts, CEO of Shell E&P Europe, Andy Pyle of Shell E&P Ireland and Rosemary Steen of EEI along with Minister for Communications, Marine and Natural Resources Dermot Ahern, department official Michael Guilfoyle, Minister for Environment, Heritage and Local Government Martin Cullen and department official Mary Moylan, and the Taoiseach's official, Martin Fraser. The meeting took place in the Taoiseach's department. Before the meeting Shell indicated that Mr Botts, a senior decision maker, was meeting the Taoiseach to assess whether the company should commit further resources to the project.

According to the briefing documents, the Department of the Environment, Heritage and Local Government assured Shell that both Mayo County Council and An Bord Pleanála would treat any new application as a priority and that Mayo County Council would be happy to continue discussions at the pre-planning stage. According to the steering note prepared for the Taoiseach, "D/CM&NR (Department of Communications, Marine and Natural Resources) are of the view that enactment of the proposed critical infrastructural legislation would address the company's concerns and uncertainties."

The Taoiseach advised the company that without certainty on the proposed critical infrastructure legislation, the company would be better off proceeding under the existing system. Tom Botts told the assembled ministers and officials that for the project to be "economic", Shell needed to start construction in summer 2004 and produce first gas in 2006 at the latest.

Does this refer to issues of the peat removal or to alternative terminal sites or what else?"

The document generated by the Department of Marine officials continues:

> "ABP's decision has had serious implications for the progress of this development in that: Unless the proposed design concept is changed e.g. to offshore, the project will be subject to the planning process for the terminal under the Planning and Development Act 2000.
>
> A new planning application and its progress through the existing planning process could take between 1 and 2 years and would involve substantial additional costs."

According to the documents, Shell, operating as Enterprise Energy Ireland Limited (EEIL), advised the government that: "As a consequence of the delay in the ABP planning process EEIL have incurred additional costs of €100 million and these will continue to increase."

BEFORE THE DELUGE

As the Shell delegation filed out of the Taoiseach's office, the rain began to pelt down in Rossport, two hundred miles to the northwest. As the rain grew in intensity, soaking into the bog, great chunks of land began to peel off Barnacuille and Dooncarton Mountain, rumbling down the hillside and sweeping away houses in the village of Pollathomas below. Locals driving home from work had their cars swept off in the mud, and the landslides devastated the local graveyard. The local superintendent described the scene as "Apocalypse Now, utter devastation". Fortunately, no one was seriously injured.

Looking at the blighted hillside the following day, locals began to take in the full scale of what had happened. One of the original planned pipeline routes went across the site of the landslide. The project developers originally planned to begin production of gas in 2003.

TOP OIL EXECUTIVES MEET TOP PLANNERS

At the 19 September meeting, Shell had requested "greater dialogue with the planning authorities, especially An Bord Pleanála", and on 23 September 2003, Bord Pleanála's top officials, including chairperson John O'Connor, deputy chairperson

Brian Hunt, chief officer Paul Mullaly, planning officer Tom O'Connor and secretary Diarmuid Collins, welcomed a delegation of the Corrib developers under the aegis of the Irish Offshore Operators Association (IOOA). Andy Pyle, managing director of Shell E&P Ireland; Fergal Murphy, president of Marathon Ireland; Lief Arne Hoyland of Statoil; and Fergus Cahill, chairman of the IOOA, made up the delegation.

According to documents released by An Bord Pleanála, John O'Connor opened the meeting by saying the board was unable to discuss any

Landslide warning near Pollathomas, overlooking route of proposed pipeline

Maureen McGrath, wife of Philip McGrath, marching in Dublin with daughters of the Rossport 5 - Jaqueline Philbin, Siobhán Philbin, Mairead Corduff, Dierdre McGrath, Máire McGrath and Máire Ní Sheighin.

individual case. The Corrib delegation then made a 30-minute presentation on "The Case for Indigenous Gas". The presentation projected that the Corrib field, coming on stream in 2006/7, would supply 60% of Ireland's energy needs. The delegation asked the board for general guidance on how a large, complex planning application might be approached by a developer and put a number of questions to the board regarding re-submissions of planning applications and adherence to time scales. Mr O'Connor replied that hold-ups could occur when the developer's application and Environmental Impact Statement (EIS) were short on information and he added that neither the government nor the board could guarantee the success of any planning application until it had been through the application and appeal process.

On 3 October, Andy Pyle informed the Taoiseach that Shell had decided to "adhere fully to the existing due process". Shell began to prepare a new planning application, involving the transfer of 600,000 cubic metres of peat from the Ballinaboy site to a Bord na Móna site a further 11 kilometres inland.

SHELL RE-SUBMITS ITS APPLICATION AND SUCCEEDS

On 17 December 2003, Shell re-submitted its planning application to Mayo County Council. Rossport residents made new submissions to the council, citing the concerns raised by the Senior Planning Inspector. On Friday 30 April 2004, the council granted planning permission. Residents appealed to the Planning Appeals Board, but on 23 October 2004, the board delivered a unanimous decision to approve planning permission.

SHELL ISSUES ULTIMATUM TO LANDOWNERS

Shell set about serving CAOs on the landowners. On Tuesday 11 January 2005, with 100 m.p.h. winds blowing onto the coast, Shell engineers attempted to enter land to "peg out" the pipeline route. Backed by gardaí, the engineers tried to enter the land of local residents Monica Muller, Philip McGrath and Bríd McGarry. In each case, the landowners demanded to see the CAOs and certificates of health and safety. The Shell engineers withdrew but, on 19 January 2005, issued an ultimatum to the landowners. Shell's solicitor asked the landowners to give an unconditional undertaking to "cease and desist from all efforts and actions" to prevent Shell's "efforts to exercise its lawful rights under said orders". Shell pressed ahead with the project, beginning preparatory work on the Srathmore cutaway bog outside Bangor-Erris, which would receive the peat from the Ballinaboy site.

SHELL GETS RESTRAINING ORDER AGAINST LANDOWNERS

On 18 March 2005, Shell applied to the High Court for an order restraining six landowners from interfering with the laying of the pipeline, and on 4 April, the President of the High Court Mr Justice Joseph Finnegan issued an interlocutory injunction until the full hearing of the case against the six. Restraining orders were granted against Philip McGrath, Brendan Philbin, Willie Corduff, Monica Muller and Bríd McGarry.

CHAOS IN ROSSPORT

In April, Shell began work on moving the peat from the Ballinaboy site. The challenge was technically formidable. The peat proved difficult to excavate. Diggers sank into the bog, and three five-axle heavy goods vehicles toppled off the road in quick succession.

There was chaos in Rossport, where Shell had erected a compound on the shore. With only one narrow road in and out of the village, and no traffic management plan in place, locals were forced to make way for trucks belonging to Shell's contractors. The project called for 70 truck movements per day into Rossport for three months. Locals were unable to navigate past the Shell trucks and confrontation brewed. Rossport residents turned to their TDs for assistance.

THE QRA AND THE INDEPENDENT REVIEW

In February 2005, independent Mayo TD Dr Jerry Cowley submitted a written question to Minister Noel Dempsey to make publicly available the Quantitative (Quantified) Risk Assessment (QRA) and an independent review of the QRA. In a written reply on 1 March 2005, Minister Dempsey stated: "Since the QRA report forms part of the deliberative process under which Shell has sought consent to install and commission the pipeline, it would not be appropriate to release the report at this stage."

MINISTER PLAYS DOWN RISK

On 2 March 2005, Dr Cowley told the Dáil: "The people of Erris, who have been compelled to have the Corrib gas upstream pipeline adjacent to their homes, are scared out of their minds." In reply, Minister of State at the Department of Communications, Marine and Natural Resources, Pat "The Cope" Gallagher, speaking on behalf of Minister Noel Dempsey, told the Dáil: "The assessment [QRA] makes recommendations for risk reduction where appropriate and demonstrates that the residual risks associated with the operation of the onshore pipeline have been reduced to tolerable levels. It showed that even in the worst case of the pipeline being ruptured and the gas being ignited, the occupants of a building 70 metres away would be safe."

The Rossport residents disputed the Minister's contention and claimed there was ample evidence that smaller, lower-pressure pipelines had

Shell began work on moving the peat from the Ballinaboy site. The challenge was technically formidable. The peat proved difficult to excavate. Diggers sank into the bog, and three five-axle heavy goods vehicles toppled off the road in quick succession. There was chaos in Rossport, where Shell had erected a compound on the shore.

The Rossport residents disputed the Minister's contention and claimed there was ample evidence that smaller, lower-pressure pipelines had exploded, killing people a lot farther than 70 metres away. In June 2004, a gas pipeline explosion in Belgium had killed 21 people within a 400-metre radius of the explosion.

exploded, killing people a lot farther than 70 metres away. The residents had become aware of at least two recent fatal accidents. In June 2004, a gas pipeline explosion in Belgium had killed 21 people within a 400-metre radius of the explosion. In New Mexico, USA, in 2000, a family of 12 was killed when a gas pipeline exploded almost 200 metres from where they were camped.

BRITISH PIPELINE AGENCY REVIEWS SAFETY ASSESSMENT

On 10 March 2005, Minister Noel Dempsey undertook to publish the latest version of the QRA along with an independent review. The job of reviewing the QRA was given to British Pipeline Agency (BPA), a British-based pipeline consultancy. The BPA review of the QRA concluded: "BPA considers that the design of the pipeline incorporates measures to contain the high operating and design pressures and has been conservative in the use of materials and integrity management procedures."

The report noted that the failure frequency data was limited to UK data and recommended that data should be used from international sources; that pipeline leak models should be included for 5mm and 100mm leak scenarios; and that pipeline protection should be increased at road crossings and to extend to the road boundary, and not just one metre beyond the road width.

THE INDEPENDENT REVIEWER'S RELATIONSHIP WITH SHELL

On 25 May, the Minister published the QRA and the independent review but within hours of publication it emerged that British Pipeline Agency was jointly owned by Shell and British

Petroleum. The commercial relationship which was revealed within minutes of the reports' release caused uproar in Erris and, almost immediately, Minister Dempsey who defended the BPA document nevertheless announced another independent review.

In a statement the Department said; "The department accepts that BPA has completed the review in a fully professional and objective manner. However, the Minister remains conscious that the association of Shell UK Oil Ltd. with BPA by means of its 50% ownership of the company will raise questions as to the complete independence of the QRA review process."

The second review was then carried out in June 2005 by AEA Technology, which lists Shell among its clients.

SHELL ASSERTS CONTROL OVER ITS PIPELINE ROUTE

On 10 June, the Shell Corrib onshore pipeline project steering committee met with their legal team at the Shell offices in Corrib House. According to documents attached to a book of "Inter Partes Correspondence" supplied by Shell to Philip McGrath, Brendan Philbin, Willie Corduff, Monica Muller, Bríd McGarry and environmental activist, Peter Sweetman, Shell's solicitor told the committee that he believed it preferable to attempt entry on the land and then decide about seeking to have landowners who refused access held in contempt. Shell Managing Director, Andy Pyle, asked about the procedures involved in enforcing the injunction. The solicitor said that Shell would have to attempt entry and that, upon refusal of admission, a notice of motion and affidavit would be served on the parties, who would then have time to review the documents before the matter came to court.

On 15 June, Shell returned to Rossport and engineers backed by local gardaí attempted to enter the lands of Philip McGrath in Rossport, Brendan Philbin in Léana Mhianigh and Willie Corduff in Gob a'tSáilín. Micheál Ó Seighin joined the men, as did Bríd McGarry. When the men refused to let the engineers pass the Shell personnel called for the police to take the names of those present.

On 15 June, Shell returned to Rossport and engineers backed by local gardaí attempted to enter the lands of Philip McGrath in Rossport, Brendan Philbin in Léana Mhianigh and Willie Corduff in Gob a'tSáilín. Micheál Ó Seighin joined the men, as did Bríd McGarry. When the men refused to let the engineers pass the Shell personnel called for the police to take the names of those present.

FROM THE BOG TO THE HIGH COURT

On 29 June, Willie Corduff, Micheál Ó Seighin, Philip and Vincent McGrath and Brendan Philbin were summoned to the High Court charged with breaching the court's interim order. President of the High Court, Mr Justice Joseph Finnegan, presided over the initial hearing. The men told him they could not abide by the court order. Mr Justice Joseph Finnegan told the men that Mr Justice John McMenamin would hear their case.

Shortly before noon, the men came back into the court. Willie Corduff told the court, "I'm begging you for justice." Brendan Philbin drew attention to the lack of independence in preparing and reviewing the safety documents. "To make fair judgement, one needs to see the whole story," he said. Micheál Ó Seighin was the last to speak. "The farms form the basis of the identity of the people," he said. "Monetary compensation cannot compensate for undermining the social identity of the people." Mr Ó Seighin argued that the issue should be decided on technical and scientific knowledge and reminded the court that the community had to fight at every step to get access to information. Patrick Hanratty SC for Shell asked that the men be "attached and committed". Mr Justice McMenamin ordered the men to be jailed for contempt of court.

THE ROSSPORT 5 BECOME BIG NEWS

Willie Corduff's fear was that, on being locked up, Shell would use the opportunity of his absence to put the pipe through his land, but as Mr Corduff was on his way to prison, sixty local people showed up and surrounded his farm in solidarity. The next morning, the Rossport Five, as they were quickly dubbed, became a national and international story.

THE CAMPAIGN IN ROSSPORT: "SHELL TO SEA"

With their neighbours locked up, there was a change of mood in Erris. People who once supported the Corrib project hung anti-Shell banners over their front gates. Locals organised a rota to man the Shell to Sea campaign headquarters, operating out of a horsebox that is parked by day outside the gates of the proposed processing plant site.

The Shell to Sea campaign, which represented the five men during their incarceration, is a loosely organised collective that also includes Dr Mark Garavan, sociology lecturer at GMIT Galway; Maura Harrington, school principal in Bangor-Erris; Padhraig Campbell, SIPTU spokesperson on oil and gas; and Mayo TD Jerry Cowley. The campaigners decided to build the campaign organically, raising support in their own community, then across Mayo and then across the country. By midsummer, several environmental activists had set up a temporary camp on Philip McGrath's land in Rossport, sleeping in a marquee and using a laptop to update the Shell to Sea website, which detailed upcoming rallies and gathered media articles.

As Mr Corduff was on his way to prison, sixty local people showed up and surrounded his farm in solidarity. The next morning, the Rossport Five, as they were quickly dubbed, became a national and international story.

PJ Moran, Tony King, Mary Horan, James Healy, Kevin Moran and Vincent McGrath in the Shell To Sea campaign h.q. at Ballinaboy

Micheál Ó Seighin, Brendan Philbin, Philip McGrath and Willie Corduff at October 1st Rally in Dublin on the day after their release

THE CAMPAIGN BUILDS

Following the jailing of the five men in June, the campaigners organised rallies in Dublin, Castlebar, Belmullet, Ballina, Galway and Sligo and smaller public meetings around the country. The Mayo rallies drew crowds of between two and three thousand people. Dr Jerry Cowley served as master of ceremonies for most of the rallies. Shell to Sea spokespeople Dr Mark Garavan and Maura Harrington, former Statoil director, Mike Cunningham, and SIPTU oil and gas spokesman Padhraig Campbell addressed the rallies, along with the wives and older children of the Rossport Five.

In Rossport and Ballinaboy, locals manned pickets and prevented Shell contractors from gaining access to the site. Two weeks after the jailing of the Rossport Five Minister Noel Dempsey announced a further safety review and requested Shell to suspend work. The company, already unable to work because of the pickets, agreed.

The imprisoned men rejected the review, saying the terms of reference were too narrow and would only replicate earlier desk reviews of existing documentation. On 10 August, Dempsey announced that he would establish a separate Technical Advisory Group (TAG) within the Department of Communications, Marine and Natural Resources, which would oversee the new safety review. The TAG consisted of Bob Hanna, the chief technical advisor in the department, Richard McKeever, assistant chief engineer in the department, and Koen Verbruggen, the senior geologist of the Geological Survey of Ireland.

The Petroleum Affairs Division (PAD), it appeared, was being sidelined. In July, it emerged that Shell had breached its consents by welding together three kilometres of pipeline at the Ballinaboy site. It also emerged, after residents raised the issue, that the PAD, which had been charged with monitoring the project, had relied on regular reports from Shell rather than direct site visits. Local residents complained to the Department after they noticed the 3 km stretch of pipeline snaking through the forest.

On 25 August 2005, Minister Noel Dempsey announced that the review would be conducted by Advantica, a UK-based consultancy owned by National Grid Transco, the UK company that owns and operates gas and electricity networks in the UK. It soon emerged that Transco had on that very day been fined Stg£15 million in connection with a 1999 gas pipeline explosion in Scotland in which a family of four were killed.

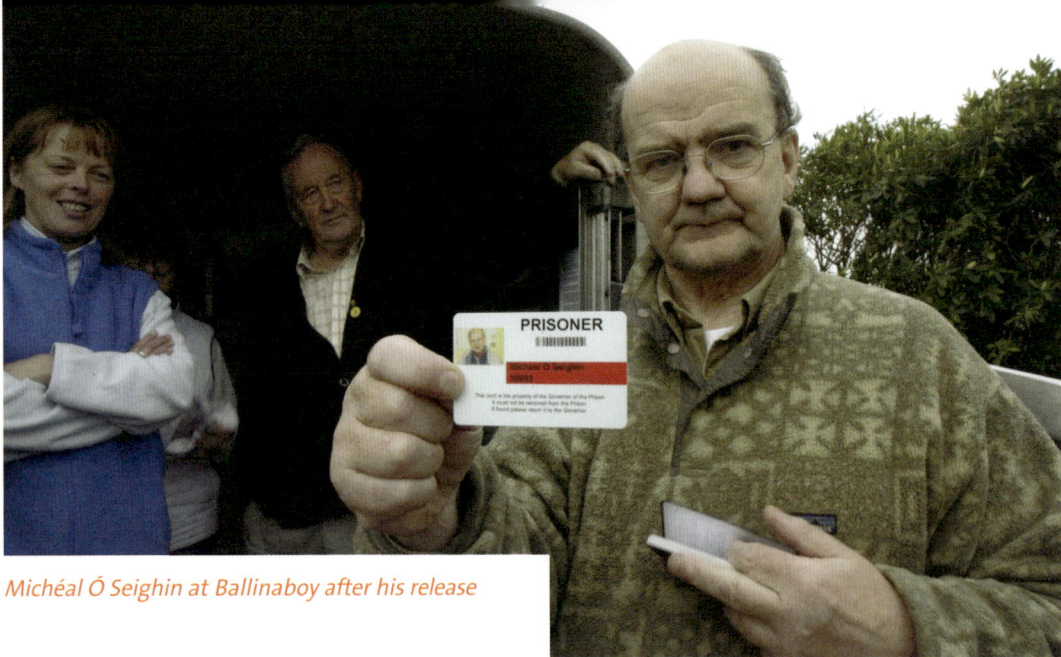

Michéal Ó Seighin at Ballinaboy after his release

ROSSPORT VISITS STATOIL
STATOIL VISITS IRELAND

On 19 September, Dr Jerry Cowley and a number of the Rossport Five's relatives visited Norway, where they spoke with parliamentarians and Statoil executives, explaining the situation. The Statoil executives subsequently travelled to Ireland to meet their partners in the Corrib development to discuss the project.

SHELL BACKS DOWN

On 30 September, the five men were summoned to the High Court, where Patrick Hanratty SC for Shell told High Court President Mr Justice Joseph Finnegan that Shell wished to have the temporary injunction lifted. Mr Hanratty told the court that a change in circumstance had occurred since the injunction had been put in place and that Shell could not undertake any further work until the safety review had been completed. Mr Hanratty

added that the company could not undertake any further work this year because of weather conditions between November and February.

Mr Justice Finnegan said that he would discharge the injunction. Mr John Rogers SC, for four of the five men, asked if the court would discharge the committal order. Mr Rogers said that an order of committal was intended to be coercive, and persuasive of purging civil contempt, and that in civil court, the court moved at the instance of the party whose rights had been infringed. When the party seeking to enforce the order had no reason to continue with the injunction, the committal to prison was discharged.

THE MEN ARE FREED

Mr Justice Finnegan said it seemed that the men intended pursuing their adopted course and asked if they would purge their contempt and undertake not to breach the court's order. Mr Rogers said his clients perceived an immediate danger to themselves and their families. "I have had precise instructions as to what to say to the court and regrettably that does not include a further undertaking. They have instructed me to say to you that they have sincere regret that they disobeyed your lordship's orders."

Mr Justice Finnegan lifted the committal order and discharged the men, adjourning the matter of the court's power to punish them until 25 October. Mr Justice Finnegan said he would deal with Shell's breach of its consent and told Mr Hanratty SC that he wanted Shell to address the matter by a full sworn affidavit.

On their release, the men issued a brief statement:

"We the Rossport 5 would like to thank our neighbours, friends and fellow Irish citizens for the loving support we and our families have received during these 94 traumatic days. In addition we would like to thank the incoming Norwegian government for their respect, support and assistance. We remind Shell and their Irish government partner that imprisonments have historically and will always fail as a method to secure the agreement of Irish people. We now call on our supporters to intensify the campaign for the safety of our community and families. The campaign has now begun in earnest."

Mairead, Marie, Willie and Mary Corduff

"We remind Shell and their Irish government partner that imprisonments have historically and will always fail as a method to secure the agreement of Irish people. We now call on our supporters to intensify the campaign for the safety of our community and families. The campaign has now begun in earnest"

Rossport 5 at Dublin Rally on October 1st 2005

THE GREAT OIL AND GAS STORY
the colonisation of ireland's offshore

Marathon Oil commenced oil and gas exploration in Ireland in 1960. In 1970, Marathon contracted the drillship *North Sea* to explore off the Cork coast. The first well drilled in May 1970 was just 200 metres from the Kinsale field and indicated the presence of hydrocarbons. The second well hit the one trillion cubic feet of natural gas in the Kinsale field. Marathon confirmed the field's commercial potential in 1973. The Kinsale gas required a small amount of processing on the offshore platform before being piped ashore at Inch Strand in Co. Cork and into the national grid.

MARATHON'S ONE-OFF DEAL ON KINSALE

In 1975, Marathon signed an agreement with Bord Gáis to supply 125 million cubic feet of gas per day for a 20-year term, beginning with "first gas" in 1979. Marathon commissioned a production platform, which was anchored to the seabed 50 kilometres off the Kinsale coast. Gas from the undersea field was processed on the platform and piped ashore at Inch Strand.

Following the general election of 1973, Fine Gael and Labour formed a government with Liam Cosgrave (Fine Gael) as Taoiseach and Justin Keating (Labour) as Minister for Industry and Commerce. Marathon had discovered the Kinsale gas field under a one-off deal with the government that senior government officials believed was heavily in Marathon's favour. There had been a public outcry over what was seen as the extremely generous deal with Marathon which became an issue during the election campaign.

51

The Fine Gael–Labour coalition watched Norwegian developments with interest and knew the Scandinavians had been tough with the oil companies.
The Norwegian government was taking up to 90% of the oil profits in 1975.

MINISTER JUSTIN KEATING SETS NEW TERMS

With Ireland about to become a producer country, Mr Keating set about developing legislation that reflected the new-found authority of the oil-producing countries. The oil companies formed the Irish Offshore Operators Group (later re-named Association) as a lobbying force.

"I remember being terrified because I thought they [the oil companies] had all the cards," Mr Keating told RTÉ's *Primetime* programme in 2001.

In 1974, Mr Keating directed that new terms be prepared governing offshore exploration in the recently extended offshore area excluding territory covered by the Marathon agreement. By 1975, Norway was a model for State participation. The Norwegians had first issued exploration licenses in 1965, and in 1969, Phillips struck the Ekofisk field on the Norwegian continental shelf.

THE NORWEGIAN MODEL

In 1972, the Norwegian parliament voted to establish a State-owned oil and gas company and a Norwegian Petroleum Directorate. The directorate was charged with management and control of Norway's oil and gas resources, building a Norwegian oil community and ensuring state participation. The parliament also established a Goods and Procurement Office to ensure that Norwegian industry was involved in the development of the resources. The consensus at the Norwegian Goods and Procurement Office was that "operatorship", through Statoil (although not immediately and not in all cases), was necessary to learn the tools of the oil trade.

In 1973, Mobil discovered the Statfjord field in the Norwegian sector. The terms of the 1973 licensing round in Norway included training requirements and requirements for private companies to transfer knowledge and competence in the development of new technologies. Mobil was required to bring Statoil in as a 50% partner in the development of the giant Statfjord field, which secured Statoil's future for 20 years. The deal started the process of training the Statoil workforce, who took on-the-job training and company training courses with the oil majors. The deal secured the transfer of knowledge from the oil majors and the development of indigenous Norwegian industry. The industry was forced to share its knowledge and technical expertise, which the Norwegians turned to their advantage to become a world leader in deepwater exploration technology.

Justin Keating

KEATING'S 3 PRINCIPLES

The Fine Gael–Labour coalition watched Norwegian developments with interest and knew the Scandinavians had been tough with the oil companies. The Norwegian government was taking up to 90% of the oil profits in 1975.

In 1975, Mr Keating introduced the Ireland Exclusive Offshore Licensing Terms for oil and gas exploration. Drawing on the recent changes in the world energy situation, the development of new resources in the North Sea and the highly profitable nature of oil production, the 1975 terms introduced three principles regarding State revenue and participation:

1. *The State, acting for the people as owners of the resources, should be paid for this resource;*

2. *Companies engaging in offshore development on the Irish Continental Shelf should be subject to Irish taxation;*

3. *Since the resources are public property, the State must have the right to participate in their exploitation.*

States use separate licensing and fiscal regimes to deal with oil and gas exploration and production. Licensing terms govern prospecting licences, exploration licences and petroleum leases. As petroleum is such a valuable resource, it is not dealt with simply by taxation. A fiscal regime sets terms for royalties, state participation, taxation and production payments. The regime includes licensing terms (royalties, state participation) and fiscal terms (taxation).

Ireland's 1975 terms included a 50% maximum participation stake in any commercial find, production royalties of between 8% and 16% and production bonuses on significant finds. The standard corporation tax rate was 50%. The terms sought to commit companies to a programme of drilling of wells at as early a date as possible and obliged the licensee to drill at least one exploratory well within three years and surrender 50% of the original licensed area after four years. Licensees failing to carry out the required exploration programme were liable for the costs.

THE IRISH NATIONAL PETROLEUM CORPORATION

The 1975 terms envisaged the development of an exploration and production company to serve as the agent of state participation. Under Section 29 of the terms, the State or its agencies could take a 50% maximum stake in the development and exploitation of any commercial discovery.

The terms stated: "There is no question of public funds being put at risk since, at the time the State decides to participate, a commercial discovery of petroleum will have been confirmed. Furthermore, the additional financial commitment is, in the total context, modest since exploration expenses represent a relatively small proportion of the total cost involved in bringing a commercial petroleum field to the production stage."

The participation terms were drafted to ensure that the government would have full access to the exploration data, allowing the government to make independent decisions about the likely success of any particular development.

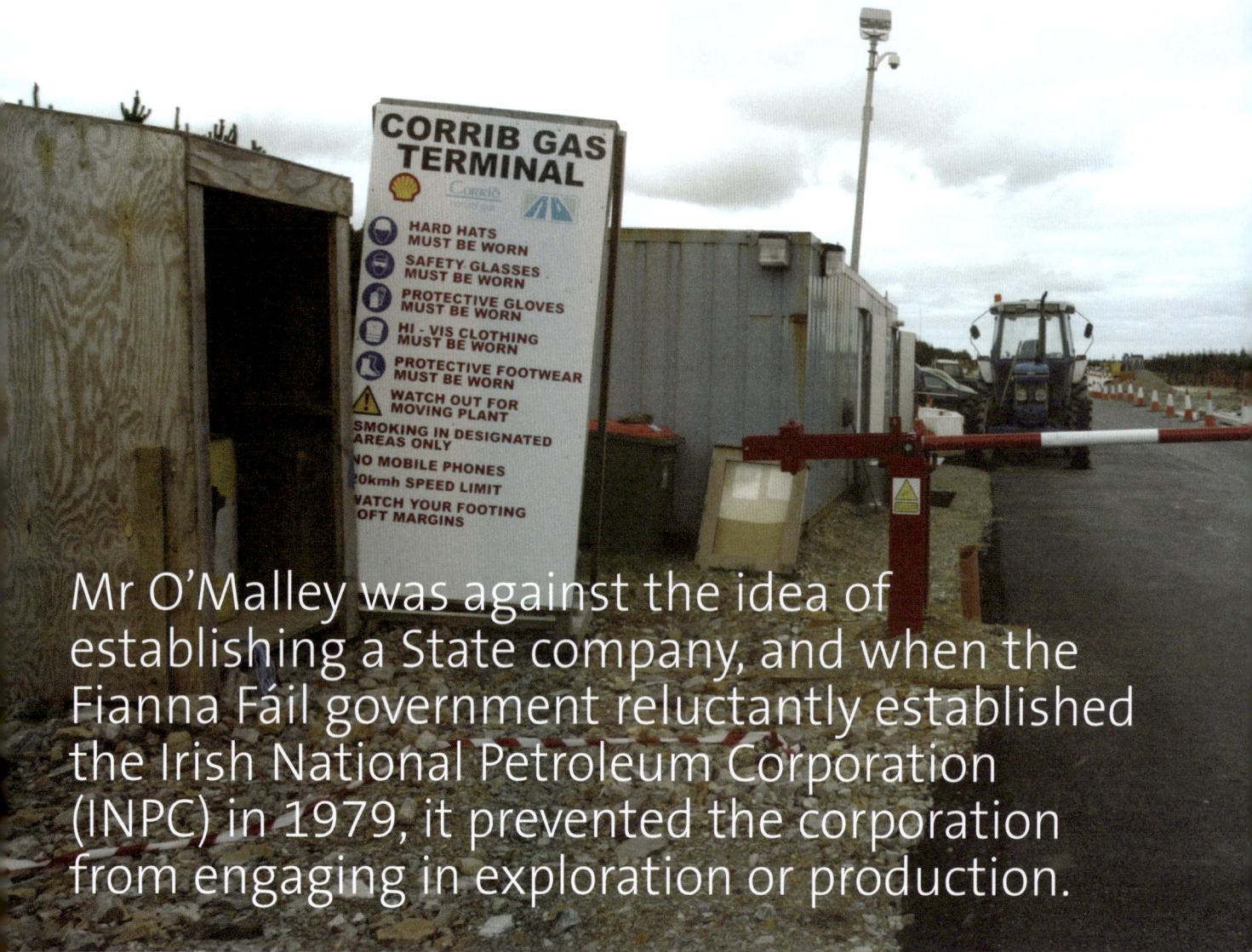

Mr O'Malley was against the idea of establishing a State company, and when the Fianna Fáil government reluctantly established the Irish National Petroleum Corporation (INPC) in 1979, it prevented the corporation from engaging in exploration or production.

A large number of wells were drilled as a result of the strategy employed by the Minister and his department officials who managed to do business with a number of the oil companies under the new terms without meeting blanket non-cooperation from the multi-nationals.

NEW GOVERNMENT, NEW ERA, NEW POLICY

The Fine Gael–Labour coalition and Justin Keating were voted out of office in 1977 before a State owned Irish petroleum corporation was established. It had not been established because no new commercial find had been made. Fianna Fáil returned to power and Des O'Malley was appointed as Minister for Industry and Commerce. Mr O'Malley was against the idea of establishing a State company, and when the Fianna Fáil government reluctantly established the Irish National Petroleum Corporation (INPC) in 1979, it prevented the corporation from engaging in exploration or production.

The 1970s was a decade of crisis for the oil industry as OPEC battled the Seven Sisters, as the oil majors were known. A number of oil-producing states wanted to do business with an Irish State corporation rather than the oil majors but were stymied by the Fianna Fáil government. Dáil records show that Norway offered exploration concessions to Ireland in 1978 on a licensing area they considered potentially lucrative, known as the "Gold Block", while the offer of oil from Iraq during the 1978–9 oil crisis finally forced O'Malley to establish a State-controlled oil company. A supply crisis and huge price hikes were sparked by the overthrow of the Shah of Iran in 1979. In order to procure much needed supplies the Irish government intensively lobbied the producer countries who responded positively on condition that they would sell to a State owned company.

Entrance to the proposed processing plant at Ballinaboy

In June 2001, during a Dáil debate about the privatisation of the INPC, Mr O'Malley said: "I have a particular interest in this because I started the INPC. It is the only State company I formed and I only formed it because I had to. I did not altogether agree with it, but I was faced with the situation in Baghdad in the summer of 1978 whereby, if I was to acquire oil for Ireland that was extremely badly needed at that time, I could only do so by forming a State oil company."

IRAQ PERSUADES O'MALLEY TO FORM STATE OIL COMPANY

Mr O'Malley told the Dáil that Iraqi ministers expressed great goodwill towards Ireland: "They accepted my undertaking that I would establish a State oil company in Ireland and that I would not sell any of the oil provided by Iraq to any of, what were then known as, the seven sisters. I honoured that undertaking later, even though a very lucrative offer was made to me by one of the

seven sisters to dispose of a substantial amount of oil I had bought in Baghdad at what would have been a very considerable profit to the Irish exchequer."

Mr O'Malley said that he had travelled to Norway in December 1978. "I went to Oslo to try to acquire what was described as a golden block in the North Sea. Again it was the same story. The Norwegians were more than willing to sell it or a lot of it to the Irish but not to any private company. In the summer of 1978, I gave directions that a State company be established. When I came back from Oslo on Christmas Eve I found that had not been done. Because of the delay, I then had to form this company, not as a State board, but as a limited company under the Companies Acts."

The INPC was established in July 1979 with a remit to pursue strategic oil supplies. It was specifically excluded from carrying out drilling or exploration.

Opponents of a State-controlled Irish oil company had pointed to the difficult conditions offshore Ireland and the danger of sinking public money into the oil business. However, the offer from Norway, had it been taken up, may well have secured the future of an Irish State-controlled oil company, as the "Gold Block" turned out to contain the Gullfaks field, which is one of the largest oil fields on the lucrative Norwegian continental shelf.

Des O'Malley

Successive Fianna Fáil and coalition governments employed petroleum consultants rather than developing a specialist sector in Ireland, and government departments dealing with exploration began displaying the secretive characteristics of the oil industry.

WHY WE ENDED UP WITH NO NATIONAL OIL COMPANY AND NO NATIONAL EXPERTISE

Ireland did not develop expertise in oil exploration and production due to the underdevelopment of the INPC by successive Fianna Fáil and coalition governments. Instead, the Petroleum Affairs Division (PAD) of the Department of Industry and Commerce, which was established in 1977, became the *ad hoc* administrative centre for the industry in Ireland. From the late 1970s, successive Fianna Fáil and coalition governments employed petroleum consultants rather than developing a specialist sector in Ireland, and government departments dealing with exploration began displaying the secretive characteristics of the oil industry.

IDENTITY OF CONSULTANTS KEPT SECRET

In May 1979, Des O'Malley refused to name the consultants to the Dáil: "In view of the commercial and strategic considerations involved I am satisfied that it would not be in the public interest to give further information in respect of these studies." During the 1980s and 1990s, the PAD continued to rely on consultants, and successive ministers refused to identify the consultants on the grounds of commercial sensitivity and national security. In March 1986, Tánaiste and Minister for Energy Dick Spring told the Dáil: "Bearing in mind the very sensitive security, strategic, and commercial considerations involved in relation to the resources in the care of my Department, I am satisfied that it would not be in the national interest to publish the names of consultants employed unless there were special reasons for doing so." In October 1987, Minister for Energy, Ray Burke, told the Dáil: "Bearing in mind the very sensitive, security, strategic and commercial considerations involved in relation to the resources in the care of my Department, I am satisfied that it is necessary to follow the practice of successive Ministers for Energy in asserting that it would not be in the national interest to publish the identity of the consultants employed in each particular assignment."

From 1975, the oil companies' sights were set for strategic and economic reasons on the abolition of State participation in Ireland. Although the oil companies regarded the oil and gas finds discovered offshore Ireland in the 1970s and 1980s as commercially unviable, people in the industry knew that "uneconomic" or "sub-economic" fields can become "economic" under the right circumstances, through a reduction in worldwide supply or, primarily, through improvements in technology.

Ray Burke (left) with Bertie Ahern in 1984
(Photocall Ireland)

HOW RAY BURKE MADE COMMON CAUSE WITH THE OIL INDUSTRY

Between 1975 and 1992, the world's largest oil and gas companies – including Amoco, BP, Burmah, Chevron, Conoco, Elf, Esso (Exxon), Enterprise, Gulf, Phillips, Marathon, Shell, Texaco and Total – drilled 100 wells offshore Ireland, but during this period the oil majors, by their own account, failed to find one single well that was commercially viable.

By the mid-1980s, industry insiders were telling *Business & Finance* magazine that Ireland's offshore resources did not contain any big fields, but only small fields, which were laced around the coast like a "string of pearls". These "pearls" were the marginal small fields in complex geological structures that the industry claimed it could not develop commercially under existing terms.

DICK SPRING CHANGES THE TERMS

The first changes to the 1975 terms came about under the Fine Gael–Labour coalition in April 1985, when Tánaiste and Minister for Energy Dick Spring introduced new exploration terms for marginally profitable fields of less than 75 million barrels. Mr Spring announced that he would reduce State royalties and introduce a sliding scale of State participation on marginal fields. In September 1986, Mr Spring announced further changes, including the abolition of participation rights for marginal fields, clearing the way for the industry to develop small offshore fields without any State participation and minimum royalties.

THE INFLUENCE OF RAY BURKE

In 1987, Fianna Fáil returned to government, and Taoiseach, Charles Haughey, appointed Ray Burke as Minister for Energy. Mr Burke, who had previously served as Minister of State in the department, entered negotiations with the oil companies, which were lobbying for changes in the licensing terms, and with Marathon, which was looking for a better deal for the Kinsale gas.

From 1975, the oil companies' sights were set for strategic and economic reasons on the abolition of State participation in Ireland.

MARATHON GOES TO COURT FOR CHANGE IN TERMS

During late 1986 and early 1987, Marathon was seeking to change its contract with Bord Gáis and the Department of Energy over a new price for its Kinsale gas, which had originally been fixed in a 20-year agreement negotiated in 1975. Marathon was selling the gas to Bord Gáis under a bulk discount arrangement, and Bord Gáis was selling the gas on to other semi-State organisations, such as Nitrogen Teoranta Éireann (NET) and the Electricity Supply Board (ESB), and to industrial customers and paying significant dividends to the Exchequer.

In 1985, Marathon took Bord Gáis to the High Court in a dispute over the supply agreement clauses. The High Court ruled in favour of Bord Gáis, and Marathon appealed the decision to the Supreme Court, which ruled in July 1986 to uphold the High Court decision relating to price but overruled the judgement relating to quantity. The judgment allowed Marathon to restrict its annual quantity supplied from the Kinsale field to 60 billion cubic feet, allowing Marathon to negotiate a new price for any gas beyond that quantity.

MINISTER RAY BURKE OILS THE LEGISLATIVE WHEELS

Following his appointment in March 1987, Mr Burke began negotiating with the oil companies meeting directly with executives on occasion and in the absence of his department officials.

On 8 April 1987, Mr Burke told the Dáil that he was considering changes in the licensing terms: "Taxation issues are obviously a matter for the Minister for Finance but I can assure the House that, in so far as it is open to me to do so and taking account of the national interest, I will ensure that no obstacle is left in the way of exploration in our offshore. At times such as this, when oil prices are low and exploration money is scarce, Governments must look at the main factor affecting exploration over which they have control, namely the national licensing terms under which exploration takes place. In that regard, our licensing terms are in general competitive with those prevailing in western Europe. I am, however,

Mr Burke began negotiating with the oil companies, meeting directly with executives on occasion and in the absence of his department officials.

having a review of the situation carried out in my Department and when that is completed I will take whatever additional steps I deem necessary to accelerate exploration activity."

On 30 September 1987, Mr Burke announced new fiscal terms that included the exemption of all oil and gas production from royalty payments, a 100% tax write-off against profits on capital expenditure for exploration, development and production extending back 25 years and the abolition of all other State participation in oil and gas development. Electing to leave corporation tax at 50%, he told the press that, after considering a reduction, he had decided that such a move would be "over-generous". Five years later, the then Minister for Finance, Bertie Ahern, cut the oil industry corporation tax to 25%.

AN "ACT OF ECONOMIC TREASON"

When the Dáil resumed in October, several TDs raised questions about the new terms. Mr Burke told the Dáil: "The reason for revising our offshore licensing terms was that I was gravely concerned about exploration prospects. Given the continuing low price of crude oil, recent disappointing drilling results and the small number of commitment wells in the next few years, radical action was called for." Mr Burke said that existing licensing terms were unattractive to the exploration companies and said he was "gravely concerned" that exploration might disappear from Irish waters altogether.

In a Dáil speech during the same month the leader of the Labour Party, Dick Spring, described Mr Burke's revisions as "an act of economic treason".

In January 1988, Mr Burke reported to the Dáil; "I have met representatives of more than 20 companies from around the world – some were

In a Dáil speech during the same month the leader of the Labour Party, Dick Spring, described Mr Burke's revisions as "an act of economic treason".

operating here before, some were here and left and others were never in Irish waters,". He added: "As well as my own contacts with these oil companies, there have been a considerable number of contacts between officials of my Department and representatives of other companies."

Mr Burke was later found to have received a number of corrupt payments during the late 1980s, and in 2004 he pleaded guilty to charges of making false tax returns. The interim report of the Flood Tribunal in September 2002 found that Mr Burke had received a number of corrupt payments during his twenty five year political career. They included a number of significant payments in the period leading to the general election of June 1989. The tribunal is still investigating a payment, during the same period, of £30,000 to Mr Burke by Mr Robin Rennicks a director of a company owned by the Fitzwilton Group which is controlled by Mr Tony O'Reilly.

DEPARTMENT DENIES BURKE CHANGED TERMS

The Department of Communications, Marine and Natural Resources has recently denied that Mr Burke had a role in changing the oil and gas licensing terms. Documentation supplied to Mayo County Council on 12 August 2005 from the office of Noel Dempsey, the Minister of Communications, Marine and Natural Resources, in advance of a council meeting, stated that there was no ministerial involvement in changing the 1975 licensing terms. According to the document, the 1992 licensing terms "developed from a comparative study of international terms, and went to Government via an Aide Memoire in September 1987."

The document also states: "It has been suggested that the changes in the licensing terms are

The entrance to the Srathmore cut-away bog close to Bangor Erris, where Shell plans to store peat from the Ballinaboy site

Pipeline constructed without Ministerial consent at Ballinaboy

somehow linked to, or are a result of, Mr Burke's period as Minister. PAD had found nothing to support this, in terms of directions (or evidence of or references to directions) from the Minister or his office. It would seem that there were independent reasons for the changes, and PAD is of the view that these changes would have had to be brought in whoever was in office."

This apparent denial of involvement by Mr Burke in the introduction of new licensing terms in 1987 is in direct conflict with the content of public statements made in the Dáil by the former minister in April and October 1987 and which we record above. It is also the case that it is the responsible minister who brings proposals on licensing terms or other matters to Cabinet for decision.

After Mr Burke's changes the new licensing terms came into immediate effect.

On 30 May 1991, Minister for Energy Bobby Molloy told the Dáil that he had asked his department to review the offshore licensing terms in light of the government decision to incorporate petroleum taxation legislation into the 1992 Finance Bill.

MINISTER FOR FINANCE BERTIE AHERN GOES FURTHER

In April 1992, the Minister for Finance Bertie Ahern introduced the 1992 Finance Act incorporating and extending Mr Burke's 1987 fiscal terms. Mr Ahern told the Dáil he would set out "the definitive tax regime which is to apply to oil and gas activities in Ireland's offshore areas, other than the Marathon acreage, and which is designed to improve Ireland's competitive position in attracting oil and gas exploration".

He added: "A particular feature is the provision for a special incentive rate of corporation tax of 25 per cent, which will apply to income arising under petroleum production leases granted by the Minister for Energy before certain specified dates. These dates reflect the respective degrees of success of difficulty of gaining access to, and developing, commercial discoveries in the offshore areas, as indicated by the duration of exploration licences granted in respect of such waters – longer licences being granted for exploration of more difficult waters."

The State then proceeded, under the 1992 terms, to abandon all principles of good offshore management.

NO OPPOSITION FROM OPPOSITION

Fine Gael's Michael Noonan told the Dáil: "The petroleum taxation provisions of Chapter VI, to a large extent, appear to be a rerun of the 1985 amendment we produced when in Government but did not enact for one reason or another and will warrant scrutiny in the Committee Stage. I do not intend to deal with them now."

Labour's deputy leader, Ruairi Quinn, said: "We still do not have a taxation regime that works to the point that we achieve significant levels of exploration that would reduce our dependency on imported oil and produce on-shore oil here. Since there is at present no tax revenue or yield from this activity, I am prepared to suspend judgment on the operation of the petroleum taxation regime and the changes being proposed in this Bill because, in fairness, the previous regime did not produce any kind of activity. Therefore, any change which would result in any such activity should be carefully examined. We will have to come back to the point either on Committee Stage or at a later stage when we have seen how it functions and operates."

Bobby Molloy prepared to introduce the new licensing terms, telling the Dáil on 5 May 1992: "Taken together, the enactment of petroleum taxation legislation and publication of the new licensing terms will, for the first time, equip Ireland with a complete regime of fiscal and non-fiscal measures applicable to hydrocarbons exploration, development and production. I believe these necessary steps will place Ireland in a strong position once again in relation to offshore exploration".

The Finance Act was passed on 28 May 1992, and the Licensing Terms were introduced in early June.

OFFSHORE MISMANAGEMENT

It now appears that, having made enormous concessions in the area of royalties, taxation and state participation in 1987, the State then proceeded, under the 1992 terms, to abandon all principles of good offshore management. Through binding the fiscal regime and permitting the alienation of vast amounts of territory for long periods in return for insignificant exploration commitment and by transferring power and rights in so many matters from the Minister to the oil companies, the State is no longer the owner and landlord of its own territory. Under the new terms, the oil companies became the new proprietors.

Mr Burke's 1987 terms were introduced in order to encourage more exploration in the Irish offshore at a time when crude oil prices were low and few wells were being drilled.

Pipeline welding equipment at Ballinaboy

The changes to the 1975 Offshore Licensing Terms made by Mr Burke in 1987 were supposed to 'kick-start' exploration and production but the government then proceeded in 1992 to enshrine the 'kick-start' provisions in a manner that abandoned all the principles of good offshore management.

Although the 1992 terms were suppposed to improve conditions for exploration, oil companies only drilled 26 exploration wells between 1993 and 2004, compared to 100 exploration wells between 1975 and 1992.

The overall effect of the 1992 terms appears to be that, even in the event of a commercial discovery, very large tracts of the Irish offshore will have been ceded to the oil companies into the distant future, tying the hands of future governments.

In the 1992 terms, it is stated: "There is a direct link between the Licensing Terms and Ireland's statutory petroleum taxation regime. Companies committing to activities offshore Ireland, can,

therefore, be assured that they will be operating in an integrated environment with appropriate linkages between fiscal and non-fiscal elements."

GOVERNMENT BINDING ITS OWN HANDS

This appears to suggest that the Government cannot change the tax regime during the lifetime of an authorisation. It is highly unusual to bind the hands of Government in matters of taxation in this way, as was done under the old Marathon agreement. Under the 1975 terms, care was taken to ensure that this did not happen.

The introduction to the 1992 terms further states that oil or gas can be delivered at 'market prices', unlike the previous agreement with Marathon where the company supplies gas to Bord Gáis under a bulk discount supply agreement. Hence, although there is to be no State participation and no royalties, and potentially very little tax accruing to the State, the Irish people will now be obliged to pay for any oil or gas from the Irish offshore at full market prices.

The fundamental requirements of a prudent licensing regime are to avoid the alienation or surrender of large tracts of prospective territory

Although there is to be no State participation and no royalties, and potentially very little tax accruing to the State, the Irish people will now be obliged to pay for any oil or gas from the Irish offshore at full market prices.

Along with the 1992 provision for market prices this means that the State will have to pay full price for gas from the Irish offshore and will have no control over prices, even in emergencies.

for unrealistic periods of time and to ensure that drilling of wells occurs at an early stage, and that companies are not allowed to sit on territory for long periods without carrying out work.

3 KINDS OF EXPLORATION LICENCES

There are three types of exploration licence: a standard exploration licence, which is issued for six years; a deepwater licence, which is issued for twelve years; and a frontier licence, which is issued for periods of not less than fifteen years. No standard licences have been issued under the 1992 terms, and only one deepwater licence has been issued, for the block that contains the Corrib field. All other licences issued since 1992 are frontier licences.

Under a frontier licence, an oil company can hold on to a very large amount of its licensed territory for more than fifteen years in return for drilling one single well. If a company then makes a discovery and seeks a petroleum lease, the terms do not require production to begin until eight years following notification or six years after expiration of the exploration licence, meaning that a company can control an area through a 15-year exploration licence (or longer) and not begin production until 21 years after the start of the exploration licence. A petroleum lease may last thirty years. However, the licensee is entitled to rely on his own data and his own plans in assessing commerciality, and the Minister must grant the lease if requested. In considering the case, the Minister is confined to the licensee's data. This is different from the 1975 terms, which did not confine the Minister in this way.

When a commercial field has been discovered, it is well known in the oil industry that an adjoining territory may be extremely valuable. In some countries, these adjoining blocks are sold by auction. This is completely precluded in the 1992 terms, as the only entity given any rights to the territory is the lessor of the commercial field.

Aerial view of the site of the proposed Gas Processing Plant in Ballinaboy (lower left) looking west towards Sruwaddacon Bay and Broadhaven Bay (photo Jan Pesch)

THE DIFFERENCE BETWEEN THE 1975 TERMS AND THE 1992 TERMS

A significant section of the 1975 terms dealt with the Minister's control over the landing of petroleum or gas in Ireland, the prior approval by the Minister of all contracts for the sale of gas, and the power of the Minister to require delivery of petroleum to specified purchasers to satisfy Irish national requirements. The 1975 terms also gave the Minister control, during emergencies, of supplies of petroleum; the regulation of production during emergencies and the curtailing of excessive production that is not in the national interest. There is no equivalent of these powers in the 1992 terms.

Along with the 1992 provision for market prices this means that the State will have to pay full price for gas from the Irish offshore and will have no control over prices, even in emergencies.

In the 1992 terms, the government stated that "the treatment of profits generated by oil and gas production compares very favourably with other countries". Industry observers agreed. The 1995 World Bank rankings of 37 oil-producing areas place Ireland among the top seven countries or regions with "very favourable" terms for exploration. By comparison, the US states of Texas and Louisiana, adjacent to the Gulf of Mexico, are rated "tough" or "very tough". Mike Cunningham, former director of Statoil E&P Ireland, told the Centre for Public Inquiry that "the Irish terms are the best in the world".

THE NEXT FRONTIER

By the summer of 1992, the oil companies were gearing up for the next exploration licensing round, and an Enterprise Oil-led consortium applied for a deepwater exploration licence for six blocks in the Slyne Basin. The licence, which was the only deepwater licence sought under the 1992 terms, was granted on 1 January 1993.

Every license issued so far under the 1992 terms is a frontier licence, apart from the deepwater licence granted to Enterprise. Enterprise-led consortia also applied for frontier licences for the areas surrounding the Slyne basin, and in 1994, the consortia were awarded frontier licences for eight further blocks. At the same time, Statoil-led consortia were awarded frontier licences for several blocks between the Slyne basin and the Erris basin. Under the frontier licences, the Enterprise and Statoil-led consortia secured 16 to 20-year licences, which could be extended by decades, on a stretch of offshore reaching from west to north one-quarter of the way around the Irish coast. The Dooish field off Donegal and the Cong field off Sligo were discovered under the first two frontier licences issued after 1992.

ENTERPRISE OIL AND THE SHELL TAKEOVER

Enterprise Oil was established in 1982 as an independent oil and gas exploration company, following the privatisation of the British government's ownership share in the North Sea oil and gas licences. The company set up an office in Ireland in 1984. Enterprise drilled only three wells offshore Ireland between 1984 and 1996. The first well, drilled in the Celtic Sea in 1986, produced oil shows. The second well, drilled in 1996, showed oil and the third well struck the Corrib gas field.

In 1987, the PAD published a report on the Porcupine Basin compiling seismic and drilling data from several blocks. The reports were sold to the oil companies for £8000 (€10,157). In 1991, a similar report was prepared and made available covering the northwest offshore basins including Slyne and Erris.

On 1 January 1993, an Enterprise-led consortium, which included Statoil and Saga Oil, was granted a deepwater licence for six blocks in the Slyne basin. Enterprise's determination not to use Irish workers caused problems, and with drilling rigs in high demand, Enterprise did not get a rig out into the Slyne basin until 1996.

IRISH WORKERS GET SQUEEZED

The Irish oil workers were well organised and unionised. Work on rigs in Irish water was well paid. Irish workers with experience on the Marathon platforms subsequently hired on to rigs in the Porcupine Basin and the Celtic Sea. By the mid-1980s, hundreds of Irish rig workers were competing for offshore jobs. "There were no unions in the North Sea, and the companies called the shots," said one rig worker still working in the industry, who asked to remain anonymous. "The guys in Scotland couldn't believe how well we were being paid."

In 1996, Enterprise Oil hired the semi-submersible rig Petrolia to drill in the Slyne Basin. The Enterprise boss in Ireland was John McGoldrick, who wanted to hire the Petrolia with a crew from his native Scotland. McGoldrick approached Emmet Stagg, then Minister for State at the Department of Transport, Communications and Energy, and said he wanted to move the base of operations to Ayr in Scotland, but Stagg insisted

Fianna Fáil had returned to government, and Minister for the Marine and Natural Resources Michael Woods endorsed Mr McGoldrick's argument that EU regulations allowed the free movement of labour. For the Irish rig workers, it was a disastrous development and the last time that many of them worked in the industry.

that Enterprise hire Irish workers for the rig or else lose the tax breaks.

Following negotiations, Enterprise hired 26 Irish workers. In October 1996, the Petrolia hit the Corrib gas field. "I don't think they really expected to hit such a big field," said one rig worker who worked on the Petrolia. "They hit a volume they didn't expect, and there was so much pressure that they had to shut down the stack." Enterprise Oil reported that the rig had encountered technical difficulties and would have to return to the well at a later date. The company, however, appeared to be secretly confident of a find, and on 15 October 1996, Enterprise Oil incorporated an Irish subsidiary, Enterprise Energy Ireland, with a registered address in the Bahamas.

In 1998, Enterprise hired the larger Sedco 711 rig to appraise the Corrib field. Mr McGoldrick wanted to hire the rig without Irish workers and claimed that Irish workers were demanding wages "way in

excess of industry norms". When Enterprise organised to bring pipes in through the Foynes base, Irish dockers decided to picket the base in sympathy with the oil workers and, in response, Mr McGoldrick approached the minister to move the supply base to Scotland. Fianna Fáil had returned to government, and Minister for the Marine and Natural Resources Michael Woods endorsed Mr McGoldrick's argument that EU regulations allowed the free movement of labour. For the Irish rig workers, it was a disastrous development and the last time that many of them worked in the industry.

OIL MOVES CLOSER TO POWER

Having cut loose the Irish workers, Mr McGoldrick and the Enterprise team opened a new chapter in their relations with the government. Enterprise Oil was confident it had a significant discovery on its hands. It needed promoters inside the government who would smooth the way for the project and lobbyists to promote the industry line.

Days after dispatching the Irish oil workers from the industry, the Enterprise team took a table at the Fianna Fáil tent at the Galway Races, which had become a gathering place where developers and business people could gain access to ministers and politicians by buying a table in the tent. Enterprise Oil, joined by their public relations contingent, mingled with Fianna Fáil politicians and party activists. The Fianna Fáil tent at the Galway Races had been organised by Des Richardson in 1994 as a fund-raising venture. Mr Richardson, a close associate of Bertie Ahern and a key fundraiser for the party, socialised on occasion with Mr McGoldrick.

Pierce Construction, which is involved in the Corrib project, and Marathon Oil both made contributions to Fianna Fáil. In 1997, Marathon International Petroleum contributed £10,000 to Fianna Fáil, while Pierce Construction contributed £6,100 to Fianna Fáil in 1999.

PUBLIC RELATIONS

Among the PR executives was Declan Kelly, a former journalist who rose quickly through the ranks at Murray Consultants and then Fleishman Hillard. Murray Consultants had long ties to the oil industry, and its founder, Joe Murray, had edited the journal of the Irish Offshore Operators Association as far back as 1976; Fleishman Hillard was the international PR agency favoured by Shell.

In late 1998, Mr Kelly left Fleishman Hillard Saunders (renamed Fleishman Hillard since April 2005) and formed his own company with Jackie

Gallagher, a former advisor to the Taoiseach, Bertie Ahern. Mr Gallagher resigned from his government position in November 1998 to join Mr Kelly, forming Gallagher & Kelly PR. They were joined by Paul McSharry, another former Fleishman employee. The three PR executives are recognised as among the top-ranking professionals in their field.

In 2001, Gallagher & Kelly sold their company, less than two years old, for €14 million. The company was bought out by international PR company Financial Dynamics. Mr Kelly stayed with the company, while in 2003, Jackie Gallagher went on to form another PR and lobbying company, Q4, with former Fianna Fáil general secretary Martin Mackin.

Mr Kelly was then involved in a management buyout of Financial Dynamics and currently serves as a director working in Dublin and New York. Financial Dynamics is Shell's external PR company in Ireland.

With well-connected lobbyists and willing political supporters, Enterprise Oil began to push for the various consents it needed to begin production of gas from the Corrib field.

Between 1998 and 2002, the Enterprise-led consortium identified and purchased the 400-acre former Coillte site at Ballinaboy and applied for approval of their plan of development, a petroleum lease, consent for the pipeline and CAOs for the pipeline route. As Enterprise Energy Ireland awaited the consents that would give legal cover to the project, a suitor was watching Enterprise Oil. In March 2002, Royal Dutch Shell made a €6 billion bid for Enterprise Oil. On 2 April 2002, the Enterprise Oil board voted to accept the takeover offer.

> As Enterprise Energy Ireland awaited the consents that would give legal cover to the project, a suitor was watching Enterprise Oil. In March 2002, Royal Dutch Shell made a €6 billion bid for Enterprise Oil. On 2 April 2002, the Enterprise Oil board voted to accept the takeover offer.

Ken Saro-Wiwa was hanged by the military government in November 1995. The trial was widely condemned by human rights organisations, and Shell became a target of international outrage.

Dr Owens Wiwa, brother of Ken Saro-Wiwa, at the Dublin rally on the day after the release of the Rossport 5, October 1st 2005

SHELL HAS A BIGGER ECONOMY THAN IRELAND

The Royal Dutch Shell group comprises over 2,000 companies operating in 140 countries and territories and employing 112,000 people. A 2005 study by the US-based Institute for Policy Studies ranking the top 100 global economies, including countries and corporations, placed Shell at 28th place. (Ireland ranked in 41st place.) Shell ranked as the largest non-American corporation in the world and fourth-largest overall, behind Wal-Mart, General Motors and ExxonMobil.

Shell operates an "upstream" business consisting of exploration and production business, a massive fleet of huge ships, refineries around the world, oil and gas power stations, distribution systems and depots, and a "downstream" business retailing oil, gas and petrochemicals.

INSIDE THE SHELL

The company is big enough to have its own full-time critics and detractors, including Friends of the Earth, which publishes an annual report on Shell. "The Other Shell Report 2004", published in 2005, is dedicated to the late Nigerian author Ken Saro-Wiwa, who led the Movement for the Survival of the Ogoni People (MOSOP) in its fight against Shell's destruction of the wetlands of the Niger delta where the Ogoni live.

Shell began operating in Nigeria in 1937 and first struck oil in the Nigerian delta in 1958. Beginning in early 1993, MOSOP organised marches and assemblies of hundreds of thousands of Ogonis, and Shell stopped operating in the region. Saro-Wiwa was arrested and detained by Nigerian authorities in June 1993 but was released after a month. In May 1994, following the deaths of four Ogoni elders, Saro-Wiwa was arrested and accused of incitement to murder. He denied the charges but was found guilty after a year of imprisonment. He was hanged by the military government in November 1995. The trial was widely condemned by human rights organisations, and Shell became a target of international outrage.

According to "The Other Shell Report 2004", Shell's commitment to human rights and development is "paper thin":

> "Shell continues to hold on to an industrial infrastructure that is hazardous to people and the environment, to operate aging oil refineries that emit carcinogenic chemicals and other harmful toxins into neighbourhoods, to neglect contamination that poisons the environment and damages human health, to endanger the survival of species, and to negotiate with local governments for substandard environment controls."

Several other communities around the world are fighting against Shell, including Shell's so-called "Elephant" project on Sakhalin Island, Russia, where Shell's $10 billion development has doubled to more than $20 billion over the last year.

SHELL IN FINANCIAL SCANDAL

A scandal also loomed for Shell in 2004. Oil company share prices are partly based on company reserves, and in January 2004 the company was forced to admit to shareholders that it had over-estimated its reserves by 23%, or some 4 billion barrels of oil. The admission caused Shell shares to plummet, and the company was forced to pay fines of $84 million to regulators in the US and UK. The débâcle led to the resignation of Shell's chairman, Philip Watts.

Following the downgrading of its reserves in 2004, Shell, more than any other oil major, needs to increase its stated reserves. Gas prices are rising, and as resources become rarer, it seems that the price will only go up to the benefit of the oil giants.

If the Corrib field is developed through the onshore site at Ballinaboy, Shell will have achieved two goals. First, Shell will have opened up a new frontier for bringing natural gas onshore in a sensitive area. Second, Shell may be in a position to charge other exploration and production companies for the use of the Corrib sub-sea infrastructure and the production pipeline to bring other gas fields ashore.

"The Other Shell Report 2004" details the fight of local communities against Shell in Sao Paolo in Brazil, Durban in South Africa, Louisiana, and Port Arthur in Texas. For the first time, Ireland joins the list of countries in the report where residents feel themselves under threat from Shell.

"Shell continues to hold on to an industrial infrastructure that is hazardous to people and the environment, to operate aging oil refineries that emit carcinogenic chemicals and other harmful toxins into neighbourhoods, to neglect contamination that poisons the environment and damages human health, to endanger the survival of species, and to negotiate with local governments for substandard environment controls".

70

THE FINAL FRONTIER
offshore ireland

As the world's supply of oil and gas begins to diminish, the demand for oil and gas keeps climbing, pushing the price of a barrel of oil from $20 in 2000 to more than $65 by the Autumn of 2005. Increasing demand is driving up the price, but another factor is that the world's remaining undiscovered oil and gas resources – outside of countries where the industry is nationalised – are in the most inaccessible areas of the world, in the deep Atlantic and Pacific waters, where drilling is risky and expensive.

OIL MAJORS WATCHING IRELAND

The potential for Ireland to control large areas of the Atlantic continental shelf is of interest to the oil majors, which are currently restricted in their ability to explore the US Atlantic shelf. The USA has thus far refused to join the United Nations Convention on the Sea (UNCLOS), on the basis that such charters undermine US sovereignty. The Atlantic Ocean may be the final frontier for oil and gas exploration as new deepwater technology allows drilling in more than 10,000 feet of water.

More than 80% of the United States' offshore territory is under moratorium until 2012, encouraging energy majors to look elsewhere, particularly the Atlantic coasts of Africa and Europe. Ireland could prove to be attractive territory for the oil majors if the government succeeds in extending its Exclusive Economic Zone (EEZ). In June 2005, the Irish government announced its intention to seek an extension of its international boundaries, with Minister for Foreign Affairs Dermot Ahern saying he planned to extend Irish frontiers 350 nautical miles offshore to take advantage of developments in deepwater drilling technology. In 2001 the West Navian

drillship drilled in depths of 1,435 metres or approximately 4,000 feet, 125km off the Donegal coast.

DEEP WATER - THE FINAL FRONTIER FOR OIL AND GAS

The deadline for countries to join the UN Convention on the Sea (UNCLOS) is 2009, and several countries, including Ireland and the United States, are due to file claims to territory far beyond the 200-mile nautical limit currently allowed under international law. The rationale behind the extended claims is the development of deepwater drilling technology that will allow oil companies to drill in the high seas, potentially opening up the deep Atlantic Ocean as a final frontier for oil and gas.

WHO CONTROLS OFFSHORE IRELAND?

The current offshore licences are divided between international and Irish-controlled companies. Shell currently holds a large share of the frontier licences, including four blocks in the Rockall Basin, and five blocks in the Slyne/Erris basins which hold the Corrib field. Statoil, which shares the Corrib lease with Shell and Marathon, is also a major licence holder, holding frontier licences in ten blocks along the Atlantic margin.

The Italian company ENI holds frontier licences in eight of the Atlantic margin blocks between the Donegal basin and the southern Slyne basin, along with six blocks in the south of the Porcupine Basin, due west of the Kinsale gas field. OMV Ireland, the Irish subsidiary of the Austrian oil and gas company OMV, holds a 10% share in the Shell-operated licence in the Rockall Trough.

Two Irish-controlled companies, Providence Resources and Island Oil and Gas, hold licences in the Porcupine Basin. Island Oil and Gas, which was founded by former Gulf Oil geologist Paul Griffiths, holds frontier licenses in four blocks in the north Porcupine Basin, which contains the Connemara field that flowed oil for BP. Island also has licences in five blocks surrounding the Kinsale field in the Celtic Sea.

TONY O'REILLY'S OIL INTERESTS

Providence Resources, which is controlled by Tony O'Reilly senior, the proprietor of Ireland's largest media group, Independent News and Media, who owns a 45% stake, has several prospects in the Porcupine Basin. Providence holds an 80% share in the 16-year frontier licences for several blocks in the Porcupine Basin in the Atlantic Ocean.

Mr O'Reilly's son, Tony O'Reilly junior, is the current Chief Executive of Providence Resources.

Providence claims to have identified a possible 25 trillion cubic feet of gas and 4 billion barrels of oil in the Dunquin prospect in the Porcupine Basin, which has not been previously drilled. Providence also holds licences for the Ardmore, Hook Head and Helvick prospects in the Celtic Sea.

In a recent interview the chief executive of Providence, Tony O'Reilly junior, said that he viewed the strategy mapped out for Providence as similar to property development.

"I view it as a type of offshore property company. Our focus is to create more value tomorrow than we have today. There is no doubt this is the best time to be in the oil and gas industry," he told the Irish Independent in October 2005.

Dublin-based independent Petroceltic holds production and exploration interests in seven blocks and part-blocks in the Kinsale field area.

Aberdeen-based Ramco Energy has interests in a number of blocks but has recently sold a number of its exploration blocks to Swedish company Lundin Petroleum, a division of the Lundin group.

In July 2005, the Department of the Marine and Natural Resources issued further frontier licences to Shell and Island Oil and Gas in a 1,650 square kilometre block in the North East Rockall Basin. The licences are valid for a minimum of sixteen years.

"I view it as a type of offshore property company. Our focus is to create more value tomorrow than we have today. There is no doubt this is the best time to be in the oil and gas industry"- Tony O'Reilly junior, current Chief Executive of Providence Resources.

TAXING OIL PRODUCTION
a global picture

In the near future, the world's supply of oil and gas will peak, meaning that more than half of all known reserves will have been used. The second half of the world's reserves will be used much faster than the first half, as demand driven by international industrial development keeps rising, especially in Asia, where demand in India and China is growing at 10% a year.

The International Energy Agency believes that oil production will peak between 2013 and 2037, but analysts such as the Swedish-based Association for the Study of Peak Oil (ASPO) estimate that peak oil may have already happened or will happen by 2008.

GOVERNMENTS THINK AGAIN ABOUT THEIR RESOURCES

As prices now seem set to stay at the current high rate into the foreseeable future, governments of petroleum-producing countries are re-examining their fiscal regimes for taxing oil and gas production. The British Treasury has been examining plans to reform North Sea taxes, including the possibility of putting taxes on a sliding scale related to the price of oil. The UK government is aware that BP and Shell have made unprecedented profits in the past three years. The increase in oil industry corporation tax three years ago from 30% to 40% resulted in a dramatic fall-off in licence applications. However, there was a record high number of bids in the 23rd UK licensing round in June 2005.

Britain, Norway and Ireland discovered oil or gas or both in their territorial waters in 1965, 1969 and 1971 respectively, but the three countries have taken different approaches to husbanding their resources.

BRITAIN

Britain initially introduced petroleum royalties and State participation rights but abolished royalties and participation in the early to mid-1980s under the privatisation agenda driven by the Conservative government. Britain, however, is the home of Shell and BP, two of the world's major oil companies, which pay tax on their worldwide operation in Britain. The corporation tax for oil companies is 40% in the UK. There is a special field-based Petroleum Revenue Tax levied at 50% that taxes a proportion of super-profits from UK oil and gas production but is only levied on fields given development consent before March 1993. The marginal government take is 40%.

NORWAY

Norway also introduced royalties and State participation. The Norwegians are now phasing out royalties but have a 28% corporation tax and a supplementary 50% corporation tax for oil and gas profits for a marginal government take of 78%. The Petroleum Fund of Norway is a government-controlled fund owned by the people of Norway that currently stands at €154 billion, according to a spokeswoman for the Norwegian Petroleum Directorate. The fund is invested overseas in a broad range of activities. The Norwegian State is directly involved in oil and gas exploration and production through its shareholding in Statoil (70%), which was originally a State-owned company that was partially privatised in 2001, and Norsk Hydro (44%). The State also has direct investments in transport systems (including pipelines) and land-based plants.

IRELAND

In Ireland, the government introduced royalties and State participation in 1975 to govern future exploration and production. Beginning in 1985, successive governments began liberalising the terms, and under the 1992 Finance Act and 1992 Offshore Licensing Terms, the government take in Ireland is now limited to 25% corporation tax with 100% write-offs against exploration, development and production costs. The Ambassador licence that taxes Marathon's fields in Kinsale and southwest Kinsale pays royalties at 12.5% and corporation tax at 35%, but due to remittance, the marginal government take is 25%.

Under the 1992 Finance Act and the 1992 offshore licensing terms, it appears that the Irish government will be unable to alter any terms for licences that have already been given, most of which are minimum 16-year frontier licences.

The British Treasury has been examining plans to reform North Sea taxes, including the possibility of putting taxes on a sliding scale related to the price of oil. The UK government is aware that BP and Shell have made unprecedented profits in the past three years.

WHAT SHELL SAYS ABOUT CORRIB

Asked to make a submission to this report a spokesperson for Shell E&P Ltd directed the Centre for Public Inquiry to the company's website which includes information on the Corrib gas project. From the website we drew the following information which we submitted to Shell for comment before publication of this report.

"The pipeline route is generally flat along its entire length and was deliberately routed on the north side of Sruwaddacon Bay – away from Dooncarton Hill where there is a history of landslides.

In the process of selecting a design concept for the development of Corrib, priority has been given to minimising hazards and preventing incidents that could endanger personnel, either public or company. The risk factors associated with an offshore platform, even one close to shore, are significantly higher when taking into account the exposure of personnel working and travelling offshore.

Subsea offshore facilities enable the field to be operated remotely from the onshore terminal. This minimises the need for personnel to work offshore, thereby reducing the exposure of personnel at work to risk. In addition, cost considerations make offshore processing non-viable for a field of this type, location and size. All options were scrutinised by the relevant authorities who also supported the onshore concept.

The Corrib project has been through a rigorous and transparent planning and authorisation process, with significant public consultation and input, during which the project benefits and impacts were evaluated.

The first planning application for the onshore gas terminal was turned down by An Bord Pleanála in April 2003 because of their concern on one issue, the management of peat on the site. The consultant employed by An Bord Pleanála had reservations regarding the long-term integrity of the retaining structures for the peat excavated from the terminal footprint. SEPIL worked to address this issue and a new planning application submitted to the local authority, Mayo County Council, in December 2003 contained a proposal to remove the peat from the site and deposit it at a Bord na Móna cut-over site 11km from the terminal site. The proposal met with the approval of both the local authority and the national

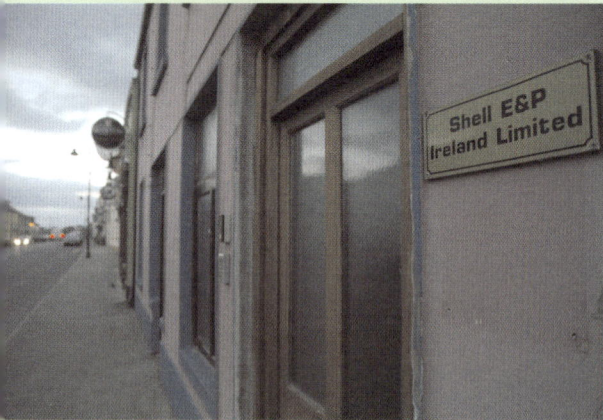

Shell office in Bangor-Erris

The consultant concluded, on the basis of his evaluation, that the pipeline had been designed in accordance with best public safety consideration and is appropriate for the pipeline operating conditions. The pipeline is a minimum of 70m from the nearest house compared to BGÉ transmission pipelines that can pass within 3m."

Shell Exploration and Production Ireland Limited said that it values local opinion, support and input as critical to the success of the project.

"We have always tried to communicate with the local community, and with the local stakeholders," said Shell spokesperson Susan Shannon.

planning board and final approval was granted in October 2004, with 42 conditions attached.

The pipeline has been designed to an internationally recognised code BS8010 (now renamed PD8010) which is at least as stringent as the Irish code IS328. BS8010 is the most applicable code, as IS328 does not cater for pipelines that run predominantly offshore, as is the case with the Corrib pipeline. The BS8010 code was fully accepted as the most suitable by the consultant employed by the Department of Communications, Marine and Natural Resources.

Asked about the estimated value of the Corrib gas field Ms Shannon said that she could not comment on commercially sensitive matters.

Shell has recently been working closely with the Pro Erris Gas Group (PEGG) which is campaigning for the pipeline and processing plant.

On 28 October, Minister Dempsey rejected the proposal from the Pro Erris Gas Group that Shell pay €250,000 to the local community rather than dismantle a section of the pipeline which had been built without ministerial consent.

CORRIB TIMELINE

1969
Marathon awarded licence for offshore exploration

1970
Marathon Oil begins exploring for oil and gas off the Cork coast and drills first gas well

1973
Marathon declares a commercial find 50 kilometres offshore Kinsale Head

1975
Minister for Commerce and Industry Justin Keating introduces licensing terms for offshore exploration and production, including provision for 50% State participation

1978
Marathon begins production of gas from Kinsale field

1979
Minister for Energy Des O'Malley sets up Irish National Petroleum Corporation

1985
Minister for Energy Dick Spring introduces revised terms for marginal fields of less than 75 million barrels

1987
Minister for Energy Ray Burke introduces new licensing terms, abolishing State royalties and State participation, and introduces 100% tax write-offs for exploration and development costs on 30 September, before return of Dáil

1991
Government publishes Northwest Offshore data compilation.

1992
Minister for Finance Bertie Ahern introduces 1992 Finance Act, reducing corporation tax on oil profits to 25%. Minister for Marine and Natural Resources Bobby Molloy introduces new licensing terms

reflecting Burke's changes

January 1993
Enterprise Oil awarded deepwater exploration licence for block 18/20, which contains Corrib gas field

October 1996
Enterprise Oil discovers the Corrib gas field 80 kilometres off the northwest coast of Mayo. Enterprise Energy Ireland incorporated in Bahamas

April 2000
First notices of Corrib gas project in Mayo newspapers

July 2000
Government passes Gas (Amendment) Act of 2000

September 2000
Bertie Ahern introduces Statutory Instrument 110, transferring powers over production pipelines from Department of Public Enterprise to Department of the Marine and Natural Resources

October 2000
Bord Gáis announces plans to construct pipeline from processing plant site in north Mayo to national grid loop at Craughwell, Co. Galway, on behalf of the Corrib developers Enterprise Energy Ireland, Statoil and Marathon

November 2000
Enterprise Energy Ireland (EEI) applies to Mayo County Council for planning permission for a gas processing plant at Ballinaboy Bridge

December 2000
Micheál Ó Seighin makes submission to Mayo County Council opposing the development

January 2001
EEI applies to Department of Marine and Natural Resources for petroleum lease. Mayo County Council requests further information from EEI

April 2001
EEI re-applies to Mayo County Council for planning permission

June 2001
Mayo County Council requests further information on the EEI planning application

July 2001
EEI submits further information to County Council; Minister for Marine and Natural Resources Frank Fahey hosts public meeting in Geesala, Co. Mayo. Mr Fahey convenes Marine Licence Vetting Committee (MLVC) to examine plan of development, foreshore lease and petroleum lease applications

August 2001
Mayo County Council grants planning permission for terminal; Rossport residents immediately appeal decision to An Bord Pleanála

15 November 2001
Frank Fahey introduces Statutory Instrument 517, giving the Minister for the Marine and Natural Resources powers to grant compulsory acquisition orders for land along the route of the pipeline

16 November 2001
Fahey grants petroleum lease to EEI; Bord Pleanála announces oral hearings into appeal against Mayo County Council planning decision

21 November 2001
EEI submits new environmental impact statement (EIS) to Department of Marine and Natural Resources in support of application to build a gas pipeline from sub-sea facilities to the processing plant at Ballinaboy. EEI applies for approval of its plan of development, foreshore licence and consent to construct the pipeline

December 2001
MLVC holds public meeting in Geesala

February 2002
Bord Pleanála oral hearing opens

March 2002
End of first Bord Pleanála hearing. Government passes Gas (Interim) (Regulation) Act of 2002. MLVC approves project with conditions. Report by consultant Andrew Johnston approves design of pipeline with minimal changes

April 2002
Shell buys Enterprise Oil. Mr Fahey issues consent for plan of development and consent for pipeline

May 2002
Mr Fahey issues CAOs to EEI. Fahey issues approval for foreshore licence

June 2002
An Bord Pleanála requests further information on the terminal application

July 2002
Managing Director of EEI Brian Ó Catháin resigns and is replaced by Andy Pyle of Shell

September 2002
EEI/Shell submits further information to An Bord Pleanála

November 2002
Bord Pleanála opens second phase of oral hearing

January 2003
In January 2003, the Comptroller and Auditor General told the Public Accounts Committee that under the original Marathon agreement in 1960, "Marathon will never pay tax in this jurisdiction".

April 2003
Bord Pleanála overturns Mayo County Council's decision to grant planning permission and cites grounds of instability of peat on site

September 2003
Landslide at Barnacuille and Dooncarton mountains. Taoiseach meets delegation from Shell. Bord Pleanála meets delegation from Shell, Statoil and Marathon and the Irish Offshore Operators Association

December 2003
Shell re-submits planning application to Mayo County Council

April 2004
Mayo County Council approves project. Rossport residents appeal decision

October 2004
Bord Pleanála approves project

January 2005
Shell workers attempt to gain access to privately owned land along route of pipeline in Rossport

April 2005
Shell seeks court injunction against landowners opposing entrance of Shell workers onto their land

May 2005
Minister Noel Dempsey admits that the
independent review of the quantitative risk
assessment (QRA) has been done by British Pipeline
Agency, a company jointly owned by Shell and BP

June 2005
Shell workers attempt to enter land and are refused
permission by landowners; Shell applies for
committal of men who have broken the injunction;
Mr Justice John McMenamin jails five Rossport men
– Micheál Ó Seighin, Vincent McGrath, Philip
McGrath, Willie Corduff and Brendan Philbin – for
contempt of court

July 2005
Shell admits to constructing three-kilometre section
of pipeline without consent; Minister for
Communications, Marine and Natural Resources Noel
Dempsey requests Shell cease work on the project

August 2005
Minister for Communications, Marine and Natural
Resources Noel Dempsey announces a further
safety review

September 2005
Family and supporters visit Norway and meet
Statoil and public representatives

30 September 2005
Shell drops temporary injunction. High Court
President Mr Justice Joseph Finnegan releases the men

1 October 2005
Thousands rally in support of Rossport Five in
Dublin

12 October 2005
A two-day public consultation organised by the
Department of the Marine is held in Geesala, Co.
Mayo

25 October 2005
Rossport Five appear before Mr Justice Finnegan in
the High Court

31 October
The Minister announced that he had appointed Mr
Peter Cassells, a former general secretary of the
Irish Congress of Trade Unions, to mediate between
Shell E&P and the Rossport residents

The Proposed Corrib Onshore System

An Independent Analysis

Prepared for the Centre for Public Inquiry
by Richard B. Kuprewicz, Accufacts Inc

Richard Kuprewicz is president of Accufacts Inc., a pipeline consulting firm based in Washington State providing "Clear Knowledge in the Over Information Age." He brings 30 plus years experience in the industry offering special focus on appropriate pipeline design and operation in areas of unique population density or of an environmentally sensitive nature. His background draws from a wealth of operational and field experience garnered from gas and liquid pipelines operating across some of the most sensitive areas of the world. These unique qualifications allow him to serve as an expert on all aspects of pipeline operation including, but not limited to, siting, design, maintenance, operation, leak detection, inspection and testing, emergency response, regulatory compliance, risk analysis, and management.

He played a key role in advising the City of Bellingham, Washington on pipeline issues following the Bellingham liquid pipeline tragedy of 1999, one of two major pipeline events (the Carlsbad gas pipeline failure of 2000 being the other), that triggered development and passage of the U.S. Pipeline Safety Improvement Act of 2002 signed into law by President Bush. He has also provided considerable input to local, state, and federal governments, Congress, and pipeline companies, as pipeline regulations have changed over the last three decades. He has authored numerous papers regarding pipelines and is presently serving on various pipeline technical and advisory committees as a representative of the public.

Accufacts Inc.

"Clear Knowledge in the Over Information Age"

The Proposed Corrib Onshore System
An Independent Analysis

Prepared for the Centre for Public Inquiry

Richard B. Kuprewicz
President, Accufacts Inc.
kuprewicz@comcast.net
October 24, 2005

**This document is based on an evaluation of information
readily available in the public domain**

Table of Contents

Table of Figures

I. Executive Summary

Accufacts Inc. was commissioned by the Centre for Public Inquiry to perform an independent review of the onshore proposals for the Corrib pipeline project, specifically the onshore production pipeline and the gas processing plant at its terminus. All analyses in this report were developed from information supplied in the many referenced public documents concerning this very unusual, highly unique and controversial, "first of its kind" project in Ireland. This report raises serious concerns about the completeness of previous key leveraging statements, misrepresentations, mischaracterisations, prior risk analyses, and conclusions regarding safety decisions driving current siting choices for the proposed Corrib onshore facilities. To assist readers first skimming this report, coloured text boxes capturing many of the critical issues are provided throughout the paper.

It is Accufacts' opinion that the current direction for this project's proposed siting reflects a lack of specialised experience, or a serious breakdown in management and/or decision processes. We find past Quantitative Risk Analysis (QRA) for the onshore pipeline not in compliance with even the minimum basic risk analysis requirements defined in the now outdated and cited design standard for this pipeline, BS 8010.[1] Given the uniqueness of this project and the incredibly high potential pipeline pressures in close proximity to civilians, easily exceeding the limits of most normal pipelines, Accufacts believes a QRA is not the appropriate mechanism, or satisfactory approach, for prudent project design and siting decisions for this unusual experiment.

For background reference, a brief explanation of why the Corrib pipeline is anything but normal is discussed. Key information is then presented that quickly dispels the illusion or myth that the 508 mm (20 inch) diameter 27.1 mm (1.07 inch) thick-wall Corrib pipe is somehow invincible to specific threats associated with high-pressure production pipelines that can cause leaks or ruptures. As a reality reference check, the well-documented "moderate" release gas transmission pipeline rupture in Carlsbad, New Mexico (August 19, 2000) is presented in the section on pipeline rupture consequences. The Carlsbad pipeline rupture graphically demonstrates the consequence potential of even a lower pressure pipeline, which failed at approximately 46.6 Bar (675 psig, or 58% Specified Minimum Yield Strength). The Carlsbad pipeline failed as a result of aggressive selective internal corrosion and other operating factors, and the age of the pipe played no role in its failure. Ironically, the pipeline operator complied with corrosion monitoring programs defined by minimum U.S. federal pipeline regulations of the time. Attempts to characterise that the Corrib pipeline cannot rupture from internal corrosion need to be seriously challenged and investigated. The corrosion pipe failure information presented in this report utilises well known and accepted pipeline industry tools.

Given the much greater thermal impact zones associated with a Corrib onshore pipeline rupture, our analysis indicates that pipeline routing should be at least 200 metres from dwellings and 400 metres from unsheltered individuals to avoid massive casualties and/or multiple fatalities. These recommended distances indicate that the current proposed onshore pipeline route is unacceptable. The large safety zones necessitated by an onshore Corrib pipeline rupture reflect the exotically high potential operating pressures and subsequent fatal radiation thermal fluxes associated with a rupture. To date, the pipeline operator has failed to adequately or satisfactorily demonstrate that the onshore pipeline will not experience pressures within the boundary conditions of 150 to 345 Bar (2175 to 5000 psi) studied in this report.

This report also focuses on matters related to the onshore Gas Processing Plant. The impact that plant siting has on factors affecting the onshore pipeline are clarified and explored. Pros and cons of gas processing plant site selection options are then presented, specifically focusing on major advantages/disadvantages of deep water off shore, shallow water off shore, and on shore gas plant processing options. We find that many of the previous statements driving the present

---

[1] BS 8010, "Code of Practice for Pipelines – part 2. Pipelines on Land: Design, Construction and Installation, Section 2.8 Steel for Oil and Gas," 1992, has now gone out of date and is obsolete.

onshore gas plant site and onshore pipeline route to be overstating the difficulty and costs of offshore alternatives, while apparently understating the risks of the onshore proposal. This is a most troublesome example of what is called "Space Shuttle Syndrome," the propensity to rush launch at all costs while downplaying or ignoring very real risks. Readers are welcome to form their own opinion as to whether this phenomenon is occurring on the Corrib project after studying this report.

Particular attention is paid to the issues of cold venting and excess flaring in gas processing plant design. More progressive governments have chosen to discourage cold venting and excess flaring practices for many prudent reasons and we would highly recommend avoiding either practice.

Additional observations regarding siting considerations raise further concerns about the present siting process and use of QRAs. Various warning signs are also identified that signal inappropriate application of QRA, even though risk analysis may be allowed in pipeline regulations. Quite simply, QRA should never be utilised to supplant experience, sound engineering judgment, or prudent management practices. Lastly, further discussion is presented on several other factors related to the impact on the decision making process when financial rewards are so great and liability impacts so small so as to rush or distort risk analysis resulting in very poor outcomes that are all too predictable. The impression of huge potential reward with little or no liability for poor decisions can cause even the brightest of organisations to make very unwise decisions.

It is not up to the author to decide which option bests serves the community. It is hoped, however, that this paper injects appropriate factual information into a process that, based on less than complete information supplied to date, appears to be rapidly losing credibility, and the confidence of the citizens.

II. This Isn't a "Normal" Onshore Natural Gas Pipeline

Crucial to any discussion concerning the proposed Corrib project onshore facilities is a fundamental understanding of the various differences in the types of gas pipelines. Within the industry there are essentially three general categories of gas pipelines: 1) production, 2) transmission, and 3) distribution. The role each of these categories plays in ultimately delivering gas to the consumer is illustrated in Figure 1.

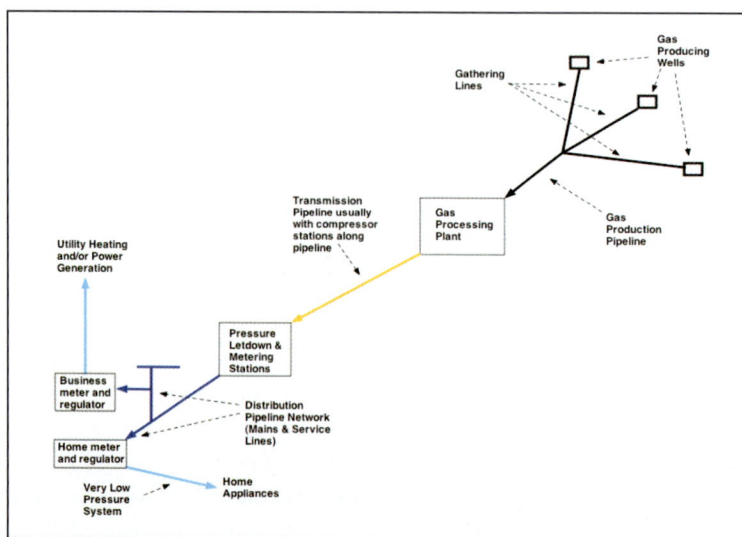

FIGURE 1. GAS PIPELINE SUPPLY SYSTEM - SIMPLIFIED FLOW SCHEME

Production Pipelines

Production pipelines, more specifically gas production pipelines, also sometimes called gathering or flow lines, are those pipelines connecting the gas producing field wells to gas processing plants that process or treat the gas to meet transmission pipeline quality specifications. Transmission pipeline gas is more restrictive in quality requirements for reasons that will be explained shortly. In rare cases, gas production pipelines connect directly to transmission pipelines as the gas produced from some wells either meets or does not significantly degrade gas moving in the transmission system. In most gas processing plants, liquid is removed and the gas dried to substantially reduce corrosion potential. Additional treatment of the gas may be required to remove certain higher risk contaminants, such as H_2S if present in sufficient quantities, to prevent problems on transmission pipelines.

Because most production gas can contain the multiple phases of solid, liquid (water and hydrocarbons), and gas, production pipelines must be able to withstand additional "reactive forces," both internal loading stresses (i.e., slugging[2]) and chemical, not encountered on transmission or distribution pipelines. As production pipelines are usually remotely located, in many countries the regulatory requirements for production pipelines can, ironically, be less stringent than those for transmission or distribution pipelines. Production pipelines vary in size and pressure based on the specific quality and operating conditions of the gas field reservoir that can fluctuate or change considerably with time in any one producing field as the gas field is depleted. Substantial variations can also occur in gas quality if other new gas fields are added into the main production pipeline, should further fields be discovered or developed. The composition of the gas in the future is thus basically unknown. The corrosiveness and toxicity of the gas is dependent on the specific gas composition and there are usually very limited, if any, regulatory restrictions on many contaminants that can seriously chemically attack, impact the pipeline, or create other problems on their release. Depending on their pressures, production pipelines can fail as either leaks or ruptures.

Transmission Pipelines

Gas transmission pipelines are those pipelines that move or transport conditioned or treated natural gas, meeting various quality specifications, from the gas fields or processing plants to the lower pressure distribution systems. Transmission pipelines tend to be larger in size, moderate to moderately high in pressure, and traverse long distances as their primary purpose is to move large volumes of non-reactive gas as economically as possible. Usually such main arterial pipelines consist of one large diameter pipeline, though multiple main pipelines can be run in parallel (called looping) to increase capacity. Along the transmission pipelines are compressor stations to re-pressure the gas as it moves down the system. Transmission pipelines operate under published quality specifications requiring that the gas carried be non-reactive and non-corrosive to the pipeline.[3] Transmission pipelines are operated as a single-phase, gas, mainly composed of methane and other minor components (i.e., ethane, propane) and inert gases (e.g., nitrogen, carbon dioxide). Odorant with a very distinctive smell is usually added to the gas in transmission pipelines to aid in the identification of possible gas leaks from these systems. Not all countries require odorant on all transmission pipelines, however.

Distribution Pipelines

Distribution pipelines consist of that network of lower pressure gas pipelines usually taking gas from transmission pipelines, at various points down the system, through pressure reducing/metering stations that drop the gas pressure from the transmission system pressure to the much lower pressure distribution system. Distribution pipeline systems consist of a grid of

---

[2] Slugging occurs when liquid periodically drops out inside the pipeline and then is picked back up by the changing flow of the gas stream, causing impulse forces on the pipeline that can be quite large.
[3] This does not mean that internal corrosion (i.e., selective corrosion attack) cannot take place, but the potential for both general and selective internal corrosion on transmission systems are usually many orders of magnitude lower than that for production pipelines.

larger diameter pipes called mains, and smaller diameter service lines that run from the mains to connect directly to homes or businesses. Because distribution systems are in close proximity to large concentrations of people, they are designed and operated at much lower pressures (usually much lower than 14 Bar, or 200 psig) than production or transmission systems. Newer modern distribution pipelines are made of steel or plastic while older networks may be cast, or wrought iron, or other metals such as copper. Because of their much lower pressures, distribution pipelines fail as leaks rather than ruptures (see Section IV Pipeline Routing Issues, discussing the difference between leaks and ruptures). Odorant is added to the gas in distribution pipelines to aid in the identification of possible gas leaks, both in the distribution system piping and in the much lower pressure home piping network (downstream of the home pressure regulator/meter) which is not considered part of the distribution pipeline system.

Gas Processing/Treatment Plant aka Terminal

Typically, along a production pipeline is a processing plant that contains equipment to process or treat gas gathered directly from field producing wells, permitting the natural gas to meet quality specifications for transmission pipelines. Depending on its capacity, a processing facility may accept more than one production pipeline. Processing facilities are usually located on or near gas production fields particularly if the gas is especially reactive. For the Corrib proposed project, the gas processing plant has, for some reason, been called a "Terminal." In this paper we will call this specific facility what it really is: a "Gas Processing Plant." A more detailed discussion of the Gas Processing Plant and its influence on pipeline routing choices is provided in Section VIII – Why the Gas Must be Treated.

The Model One Syndrome

Because of the deep water (350 metres) and severe location of the Corrib producing field (approximately 80 kilometres into the Atlantic Ocean off the west coast of Ireland), the operators have proposed to site the gas field wells on the ocean floor (subsea) eliminating the

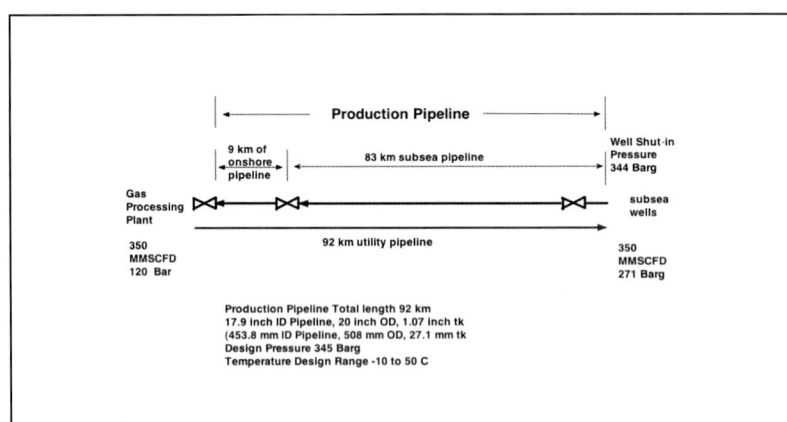

FIGURE 2. CORRIB PIPELINE DESIGN BASIS

need (and significant expenses) of a deep-water offshore platform. Figure 2 briefly summarises the proposed Corrib pipeline system design basis.

The current Corrib design proposal gathers the production gas from various subsea producing wells into a 92 kilometre production pipeline, consisting of approximately 83 kilometres of 508mm (20 inch OD) offshore underwater pipeline and approximately 9 kilometres of similar onshore pipeline to the onshore Gas Processing Plant. In addition, a utility pipeline runs parallel to the gas production pipeline. The utility pipeline will contain a package of smaller separate pipes containing: 1) a methanol/corrosion inhibitor cocktail for injecting into the

4

production pipeline near or at the wellheads, 2) hydraulic fluid to drive well head valve operation, and 3) communication fibre optics for gas field data relay.

What makes this pipeline proposal highly unique is the long production pipeline, very high, even exotic, pressures, and onshore siting in close proximity to population (e.g., the citizens of Rossport; see Figure 3 Onshore Pipeline Route Through Rossport).

FIGURE 3. ONSHORE PIPELINE ROUTE THROUGH ROSSPORT

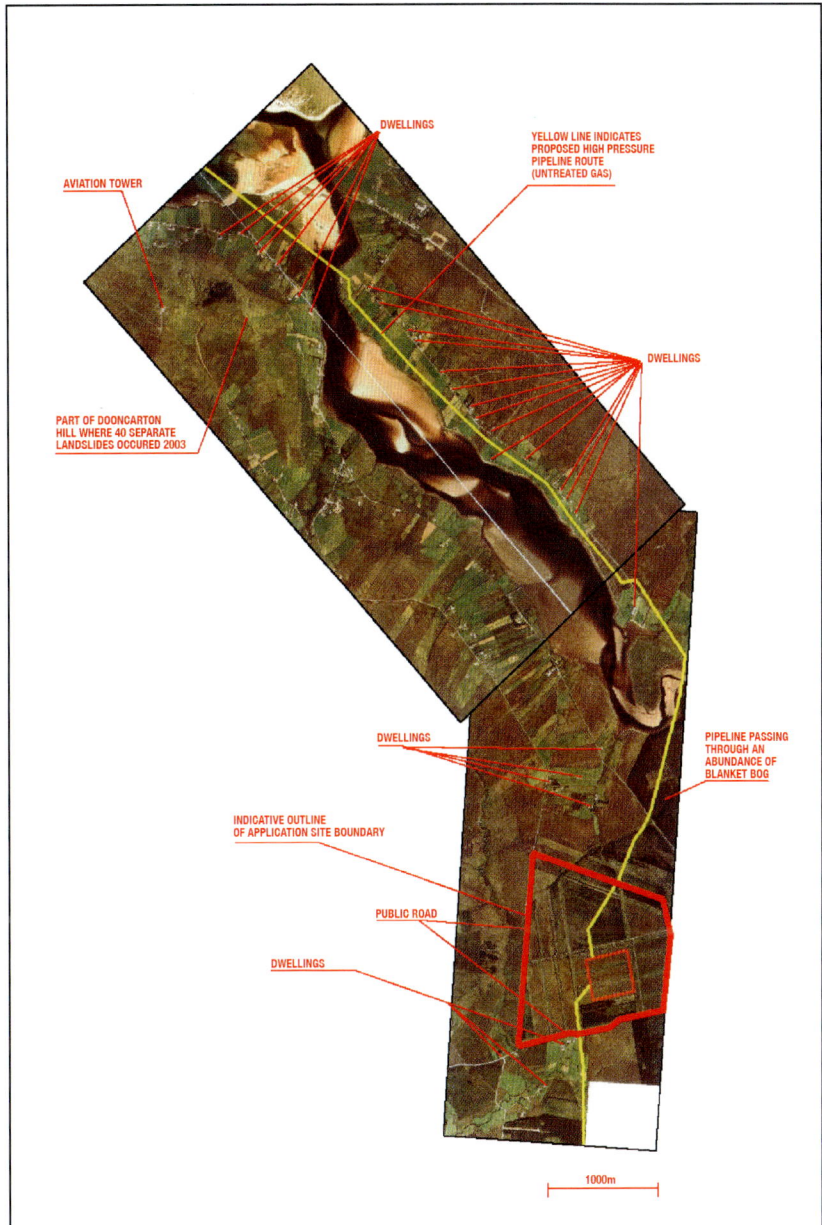

It would be fair to assume that this is the first design of its kind or the "model one" for Ireland. One would expect that given the uniqueness of this project, critical information related to specific design, operational, and routing issues would be forthcoming. Unfortunately, inconsistent and conflicting answers (such as expected onshore maximum operating pressure) have only served to increase local concerns and apprehensions about this project. Further information included in this report should serve to raise more questions from the public about past information presented for this proposed project.

Given a detailed review of the many documents describing the pressures for the pipeline system, we would surmise that the onshore segment has a very high probability, or a certainty, to reach or exceed 150 Bar, and a much lesser probability, though not zero, to attain 345 Bar pressures. Since the pipeline operator is not restricted to physically limiting onshore pipeline pressures to lower than 150 Bar, nor has any adequate design to avoid such overpressure been released, prudence would indicate a high likelihood of future onshore pipeline operating pressures reaching the levels between 150 to 345 Bar, much more than suggested by past public documents on this matter. As a result, this paper will benchmark further discussion on the 150 and 345 Bar operating pressures as boundary conditions to illustrate important concepts that should be considered for this pipeline whatever the future holds for pressures for possible offshore gas field development.

III. Onshore Pipeline Design Key Issues

There are several key issues that play a critical role in informed decision making related to onshore pipeline design, operation, and siting. It is very important for both decision makers and the public to understand these fundamental issues and how they influence the safety of a pipeline. Many pipeline parameters, such as CO_2 composition, operating pressure or temperature, are <u>not</u> truly restricted, so a wide range in these variables is possible, even allowed. Once the pipeline has been installed, many critical assumptions as demonstrated in further detail in this report, can change and seriously increase the risk of failure for the onshore systems. Failure to incorporate these many potential operating changes, which are much more varied for production pipelines than their cousin transmission pipelines, can be regarded as reckless as these changes can accelerate pipeline failure. As will be soon demonstrated, any pipeline break at these pressures can be very unforgiving.

> The maximum pressure this pipeline is permitted to experience has not been clearly demonstrated.

Should any present or future operating changes (e.g., pressure) place the pipeline into a failure scenario, no pipeline regulations or standards would necessarily have been violated. For example, flow rate, gas composition, and temperature can change in a manner that can seriously affect internal corrosion (i.e., additional fields connected to the production pipeline). All too often QRAs fail to properly incorporate future changes into the base case design premise resulting in an incomplete or improper risk finding of no significance. Any risk analysis should be clearly able to define its basis and identify critical variables that are leveraging to a risk call. Many of these important factors usually aren't as significant a problem for transmission pipelines because of their more restrictive gas quality specification limitations.

Pressure and SMYS (Specified Minimum Yield Strength)

While the impact that pressure plays on pipelines is somewhat obvious to most people, a second related and important factor is not commonly understood, even by many pipeline operators: SMYS (or Specified Minimum Yield Strength).[4] In order to perform a proper pressure analysis on modern pipeline steel, the operating pressure and SMYS are needed (along with wall thickness and approximate pipe metal toughness) to define the containment capabilities of any pipe during its operation. Despite possible claims to the contrary, these basic factors apply whether the pipe is thin-walled or thick-walled, at least the thick-wall pipe proposed for this pipeline. All pipelines have anomalies. Flaws and anomalies exist in pipelines, even pipelines that have undergone strenuous hydrotesting.[5] Hydrotesting removes or filters out larger anomalies but leaves smaller anomalies (the higher the test pressure, the smaller the remaining anomaly). Most anomalies are not an issue of concern, but some, such as those that are corrosion influenced, can become problematic for various reasons over the life of a pipeline. Pressure in relation to SMYS plays a critical role in characterising if and how a pipe will fail, either as a leak or a rupture. Leaks are releases where the through wall failure in a pipe remains essentially fixed or very close to its original size. Ruptures represent failure dynamics associated with high stress steel pipelines where the original through wall pipe failure goes unstable and rapidly (in microseconds) propagates down the pipeline, enlarging the initial failure as the pipe shrapnels (usually resulting in a full bore release or its equivalent).

---

[4] SMYS is a quality specification of the pipe, defined or usually specified at the time of its manufacture. The SMYS of the Corrib pipe is 70,000 psi (482 N/mm^2).

[5] An anomaly is any imperfection in pipe wall or weld. All pipelines contain anomalies and many anomalies are not of concern. The purpose of a hydrotest is to remove anomalies that can fail at the hydrotest pressure. The key is to maintain control of or avoid aggravating anomalies that remain after a hydrotest that could grow and then fail at pressures much lower than the hydrotest. Hydrotesting thus has limits in its application to control certain anomalies.

Depending on the four characteristics mentioned above, graphs can be developed for a pipeline that define anomalies that can be tolerated (i.e., usually won't fail), their method of failure (leak or rupture), and, in some cases, estimated time to failure for time dependent anomalies.[6] Not all anomalies are time dependent (e.g., some are stable and then become time dependent and vice versa), as their classification depends on the pipeline and its operating characteristics, which can also change over time.

No pipeline, regardless of wall thickness, is impervious to failure. Attempts to characterise thick-walled pipe as somehow invincible or better than thin-walled pipe appear to be incomplete efforts to deceive an uninformed government, public, or management team.

Such a series of graphs for corrosion have been developed and will be discussed in the following segment in this section describing, in detail, internal and external corrosion issues. Depending on the anomaly, thick-wall pipe can be even more susceptible to certain issues that can result in rupture or full bore releases than thin-walled pipe and vice versa. Risk analysis that portrays the myth of thick-walled pipe invincibility or superiority over thin-walled pipe usually misses the very real difficulties that can threaten the very integrity of onshore highly stressed thick-walled pipe. The choice of either thick-walled or thin-walled pipe depends on many factors specific to a particular pipeline operation and design, as well as its location.

Generally, and I emphasis this key word as there are some important exceptions, steel pipelines operating below 25 - 30% of SMYS will fail as leaks rather than ruptures. For example, requirements in BS 8010[7] establish that pipelines in most higher population density classification areas (i.e., Class 2 and Class 3, and high potential loading areas such as road crossings) incorporate a design factor (a maximum operating stress) for safety of 30% SMYS, and the preponderance (there are exceptions) of such failures in these lower design factor, low stress areas are leaks rather than ruptures.

When reviewing any pipeline system, it is important to evaluate the downstream and upstream facilities to assess their potential to place the interconnecting pipeline system under high pressures that can result in high stress levels and cause anomalies in the pipe to fail. Any downstream facility design that can close or block in the pipeline, or that overemphasizes reliance on electronic safeties to prevent overpressure events, needs to be carefully scrutinized as the potential for such electronics to fail when most needed can be very high and the consequences severe. In addition, upstream systems that can place any pipeline into high stress scenarios from elevated pressures must also be carefully reviewed. It is especially important that designers not rely on flow dynamics (i.e., pressure drop associated with fluid flow and pipe resistance) to prevent excessive pressure. The potential for a pipeline to reach various pressures must be evaluated from the entire system point of view including the production wells, the offshore pipeline, onshore pipeline, and gas plant processing facility. To date we find descriptions of this system on this critically important pressure matter to be seriously incomplete. This is an acute deficiency given the exotic potential pressures liable to occur on the pipeline and the extreme consequences associated with a failure in close proximity to people.

The design concept to prevent onshore pipeline overpressure has not been clearly demonstrated or communicated to the public.

[6] Estimated time to failure usually incorporates very large safety margins because of major uncertainties associated with critical measurements of key variables.
[7] Ibid., BS 8010.

Gas Composition

Gas composition factors are especially important on production gas pipelines as composition can seriously impact the operability of a pipeline, especially the pipeline's integrity. Critical composition issues include:

Wet Gas Versus Dry Gas

It is extremely unusual for gas produced from a gas field to be in a dry state. The presence of water is almost always assured. Gas containing water is classified as "wet gas" and brings with it certain risks to a pipeline operation. Water is required for internal corrosion on pipelines to occur. In addition, water or other liquid slugs can seriously change loading stresses on a pipeline. As mentioned earlier, slug catchers (large catch vessels to trap liquids) are placed along production gas pipelines. The settlement of water in low points in production pipelines can also serve to concentrate and accelerate selective internal corrosion attacks that can occur much faster than general corrosion. As a result, over emphasis on a general corrosion allowance to protect a pipeline can be ineffective at preventing pipeline failure from selective rapid corrosion attack, especially on production pipelines most at risk from such occurrences.

Gas Components Other Than Methane

Components other than methane in produced gas can have serious impacts on production pipelines. Carbon dioxide and certain sulphur compounds (e.g., COS, H_2S) in the presence of water can lead to acid attack and internal corrosion. Heavier components, such as propane butane and heavier (C5+) will also tend to form liquids and periodically drop out along the pipeline adding to loading stresses associated with liquid slugging. As mentioned previously, it is important to realise that the stated design components and gas composition may not necessarily be the same as the field ages, or if a new gas field is brought on line and tied into the same production pipeline. These changes can affect the internal corrosion rate as well as the internal corrosion potential on the pipe.

Temperature

Temperature can play a role in basically two areas. Higher temperatures can rapidly increase the corrosion rate, especially for selective corrosion attack, decreasing time to failure estimates from corrosion. The effect of temperature on rate can be better understood by reviewing Figure 4 in the internal corrosion discussion in the next section. Lower temperatures, depending on gas composition, can increase the probability of hydrate (a solid) formation that can lead to plugging of the pipeline and/or operating equipment while reducing the corrosion rate. Methanol injection should inhibit the formation of hydrates that might pose a problem on this system. The design temperature range on this pipeline has been stated as -10 to +50 °C. The onshore pipeline should not see the upper temperature range realised at the wellhead, but even at the lower temperatures expected to be encountered onshore, internal corrosion can be a serious risk. Remarkably, there is no mention in any of the public documents of monitoring the critically important temperature as it enters the onshore pipeline segment.

Corrosion Issues

Pipeline design considerations should properly address both internal and external corrosion potentials. We have previously indicated the pitfalls of relying on a corrosion allowance especially for selective corrosion attack. Internal corrosion prevention has advanced over the years, but over reliance on corrosion inhibitor programs can prove a serious mistake. External corrosion design has also advanced considerably in the past forty years. Despite all the advances in internal and external corrosion technology, there is still no steel pipeline that is corrosion free.

Internal Corrosion

To underscore the sensitivity of CO_2 composition and temperature on internal corrosion, Figure 4 plots CO_2 internal corrosion growth rates (in mm/yr) as a function of temperature for steel pipe using two models as indicated. One version generates a series of three curves for various pressures using a Norsak M-608 model; and the other single comparison curve is developed using a model from the University of Tulsa Erosion/Corrosion Research Center. It should be noted that variations in gas composition and temperature can significantly change the corrosion rates plotted, but the curve shapes won't change significantly, just shift their positions left or right affecting the "call" for the mm/yr corrosion rate. None of these plots suggest a corrosion allowance of 1 mm over the life of the pipeline for the temperature,

FIGURE 4. INTERNAL CORROSION RATE ESTIMATES VS. TEMPERATURE

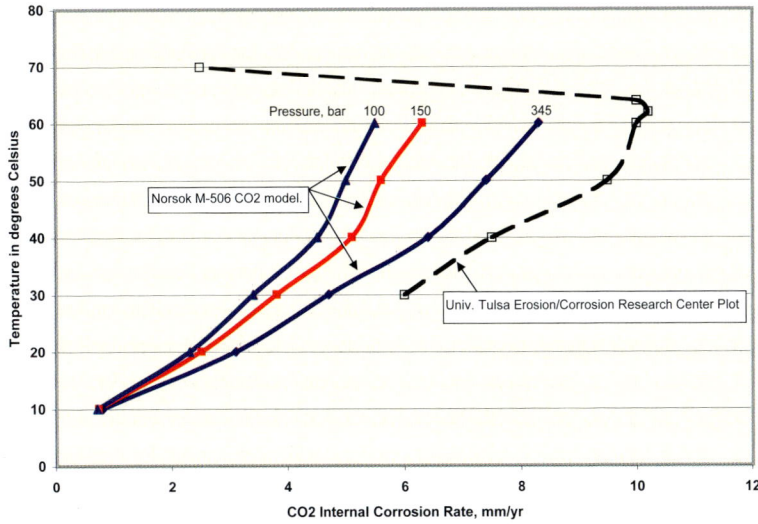

pressure, or composition ranges suggested for this pipeline. It would also be most unwise to expect corrosion inhibitor injections to be 100 percent effective in preventing corrosion on a production pipeline. This author is not attempting to cast aspersions on or support for any corrosion rate model, just strongly suggesting that the application of any modeling and reality can be very different. This is especially true if a model's application fails to adequately capture fast acting selective corrosion attack because of composition or operational changes.

To underscore the importance of not being overly optimistic about underestimating internal corrosion rate for gas production pipelines, the graph in Figure 5 has been developed.

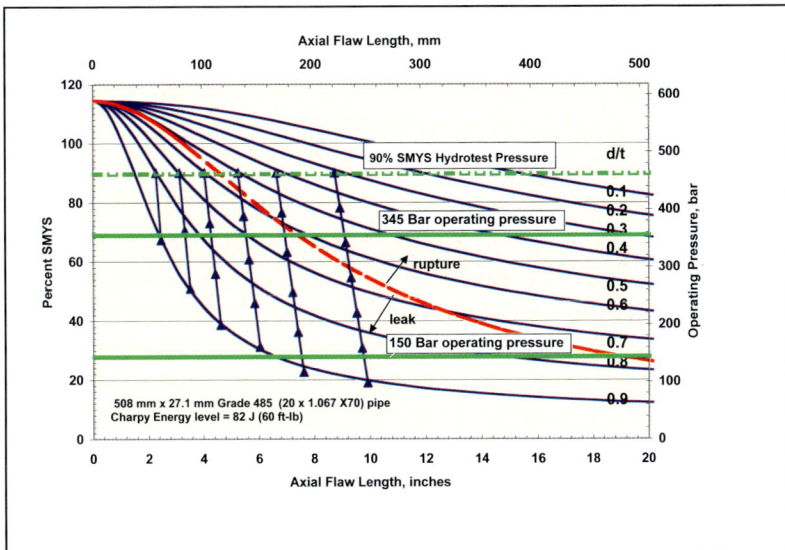

FIGURE 5. PIPE FAILURE HOOP STRESS VS. CORROSION FLAW SIZE – CO2 INTERNAL CORROSION RATE OF 2.5 MM/YR (0.098 INCH/YR)

This graph, known as a pipeline corrosion flaw growth plot, was developed utilising a well established industry recognized pipe flaw failure program (PTFLAW) that predicts corrosion related failures on steel pipelines. This figure illustrates corrosion influence on anomaly flaw lengths and depths that a steel pipeline can tolerate at various stress levels. Figure 5 is for the Corrib pipeline, a 508 mm by 27.1 mm Grade 485 pipe. A fracture toughness that maximises the flaw tolerance (tougher pipe will not tolerate longer or deeper flaws) was chosen at a Charpy Energy of 82 J (60 ft-lb). If the pipe toughness is markedly lower, the flaw tolerance will slowly decrease resulting in failure at smaller flaw sizes than indicated in the figure. Figure 5 may appear a little busy so additional discussion is warranted for such an important graph. This corrosion tool will also be utilised in the next section discussing external corrosion.

On the vertical or Y-axis, the hoop stress is indicated as a percentage of SMYS (left axis) and operating pressure (right axis), versus the axial flaw length (the most critical flaw orientation) on the horizontal or X-axis. Overlaid across the chart are various downward sloping thin line curves representing flaw or anomaly depth as a ratio of flaw depth to pipe wall thickness, or d/t. For reference, three straight green horizontal lines across the chart represent pipe stress levels at the minimum hydrotest pressure of 90% SMYS (the dashed green line), an operating pressure limitation of 345 Bar, and 150 Bar, respectively (the solid green lines). Hoop stress and operating pressure are directly related. The small blue triangles represent the flaws after each year's assumed corrosion rate of 2.5 mm/yr that initially just survived the hydrotest (the first blue triangle in each series is time = 0 which is hydrotest time) at various d/ts. The specified corrosion rate of the flaws (both in depth and in length) in this case is assumed to be 2.5 mm/yr (based on the earlier Figure 4 Norsak curve for 150 Bar pressure and 20 °C). Lastly, the bold dashed red sloping curve line represents the transition point from leak to rupture. Corrosion flaws that develop to the right and above this red line will fail as ruptures and those that fall below and to the left will fail as leaks when the blue flaw growth indicators fall on or below the pressure ranges (150 to 345 Bar) indicated. This is a lot to work through so an example may help to gain a better understanding. Some important general observations about this graph will then be made.

Looking at the top right hand series of almost vertical blue triangles, the first uppermost triangle of this series indicates that at the hydrotest of 90%SMYS (dashed green line), a flaw that has a depth of 0.3 X 27.1 mm (d x t) = 8.13 mm and is almost 9 inches long could exist (doesn't mean there is one) and survive the hydrotest. Since each additional triangle represents a year's worth of corrosion growth at the stated corrosion rate of 2.5 mm/yr it would take 2 years for this particular flaw to grow to where a pressure spike of 345 Bar would cause failure and this failure would be a rupture as the growth flaw is to the right (upper part) of the leak/rupture transition curve. Following the triangle line for this same flaw series, another 3 triangles down or 3 additional years of corrosion could occur before a pressure spike of 150 Bar or slightly above would cause failure, and this failure would be as a leak. Another way to look at this, should this same initial flaw exist and if the operating pressure spikes above 150 Bar after approximately 5 years of corrosion, the pipe will fail. If the pressure goes much higher than 150 Bar, time to failure will be shorter than 5 years with the time and type of failure (leak or rupture) depending on how high the pressure spiked and the anomaly size at the time of failure.

> The main point to be appreciated is that the pressure has to only hit once to cause pipe failure if the wrong size anomaly is present.

Because engineers often start to believe their models actually calculate exact time to failure, several additional points need to be made about Figure 5. Anomalies that survive a hydrotest will most likely be above rather than on the 90% SMYS (the dashed green line) suggesting a slightly longer time to failure from internal corrosion growth. Complicating this conclusion, however, is the proposed plan to allow the pipeline to sit in hydrotest water (probably inhibited with chemical) for approximately one year.[8] We do not advise this procedure as even inhibited hydrotest water can act as an internal corrosion activator, increasing corrosion and shortening time to failure at selective pipeline wall sites. Because of various uncertainties, variations in time to flaw growth failure are in all probability plus or minus several years. If fatalities can result from failure, one would be very unwise to operate by testing the operating pressures in the uncertainty time range suggested by the plots. Each blue linked triangle series is just for illustration purposes as the specific anomaly may not exist, though bear in mind that no pipeline is anomaly free. For example, we could have illustrated an additional, almost parallel, blue triangle series for d/t of 0.1 or 0.2 to this already busy chart that would have shown flaws that could grow to rupture. In reality there is an infinite series of almost parallel lines representing a wide range of anomalies that can survive a hydrotest (some of these are manufacturing related, others are not). Initial anomalies that are deep and short in length can grow to leak failures, while initial shallow and long anomalies can grow to rupture failure.

FIGURE 6.   CORRIB PIPELINE IN OUTSIDE STORAGE

For those who may foolishly deny that such shallow long anomalies can't exist on a modern pipeline, Figure 6 is a photograph of the Corrib pipeline segments stored prior to installation. While not attempting to raise undue alarm, the shallow long rust sites on these pipe segments could be considered precursors to internal corrosion sites. For those who may continue to deny internal corrosion is a possibility, or the specific attack shown is just mill scale, how long has this pipe been stored in the Irish climate?

To add to the above points, remember that there is a plan to keep this pipeline sitting under hydrotest water for a year. In all fairness the internal corrosion rate can be lower than the 2.5 mm/yr rate indicated in Figure 5, or it can be much greater. Any risk assessment that assumes the internal corrosion rate is unfavourably low because of corrosion inhibitor effectiveness on a production pipeline operating at exotically high pressures in the presence of local civilians, is in the realm of the recklessness.

The need for high confidence that the selective internal corrosion rate on any pipelines system is understood and under control is critical on a production pipeline.[9] To date, information from various Corrib pipeline public documents suggests: 1) an over reliance on injection of corrosion inhibitor in combination with corrosion coupons, 2) no cleaning pig program, and 3) a less than detailed smart pigging program. As a result, little confidence is instilled that the operator will have sufficient control on internal corrosion, especially if aggressive metal attack occurs. This observation is supported by further operator comments suggesting serious misunderstandings or deficiencies concerning cleaning and smart pigging programs discussed later in this report. (See Section VI Operational and Maintenance Issues of Concern).

---

[8] Andrew Johnson, "Corrib Gas Pipeline Project – Report on Evaluation of Onshore Pipeline Design Code," March 28, 2002.
[9] There is usually a very large difference in rate between faster selective corrosion attack and much slower general corrosion attack.

Important Conclusions Derived from Figure 5

1) Thick-walled pipe is not invincible to internal corrosion failure, either leak or rupture.
2) A clear understanding of the aggressive and highly selective internal corrosion rate on a particular system is very critical.
3) Faster corrosion rates significantly spread out the triangles for any original flaw and can seriously reduce the years to pipeline failure, either leak or rupture, from internal corrosion.
4) Various factors unique to production pipelines can introduce uncertainty in internal corrosion rates and time to failure by several years, either shortening or lengthening time to failure.
5) The influence of wet gas composition and temperature changes on internal corrosion rates needs to be reliably tracked and monitored for sensitive pipeline segments. Inhibitor and corrosion coupon programs can be very ineffective.

External Corrosion

A similar prediction for external corrosion of the Corrib pipeline can be developed as indicated in Figure 7. The parameters are the same as that described for Figure 5 with the exception that external corrosion rate for the one-year growth triangles is calculated using 0.25 mm/yr corrosion rate (or one tenth the rate of internal corrosion illustrated in Figure 5). External corrosion rates typically range from 0.152 to 0.305 mm/yr (0.006 to 0.012 inches/yr). A corrosion rate of 0.25 mm/yr would be a conservative rate for a well-coated new pipeline.

Comparable observations can be made from Figure 7 that were followed for Figure 5. The major point is that thick-walled pipe is not invincible from external corrosion attack failure, though because of the much slower rates, time to failure is much greater. We have a higher degree of confidence in estimating external corrosion rates for a new pipeline, but a much lower degree of confidence (if any) that internal corrosion rates will be as low as implied by previous publicly released documents for this proposed pipeline.

Following an approach similar to that described in Figure 5 and looking at the left most column or series of triangles, a flaw initiating at a d/t of .8 with a length of slightly over fifty mm (two inches) could have survived the hydrotest and would be expected to grow for approximately 10 years and still be able to just survive an operating pressure of 345 Bars. While not indicated, this same flaw could take an additional 20 years of external corrosion (for a predicted service life of 30 years) before it failed if pressure were limited to a maximum of 150 Bars. Failure of this specific anomaly at 150 Bars would be as a leak.

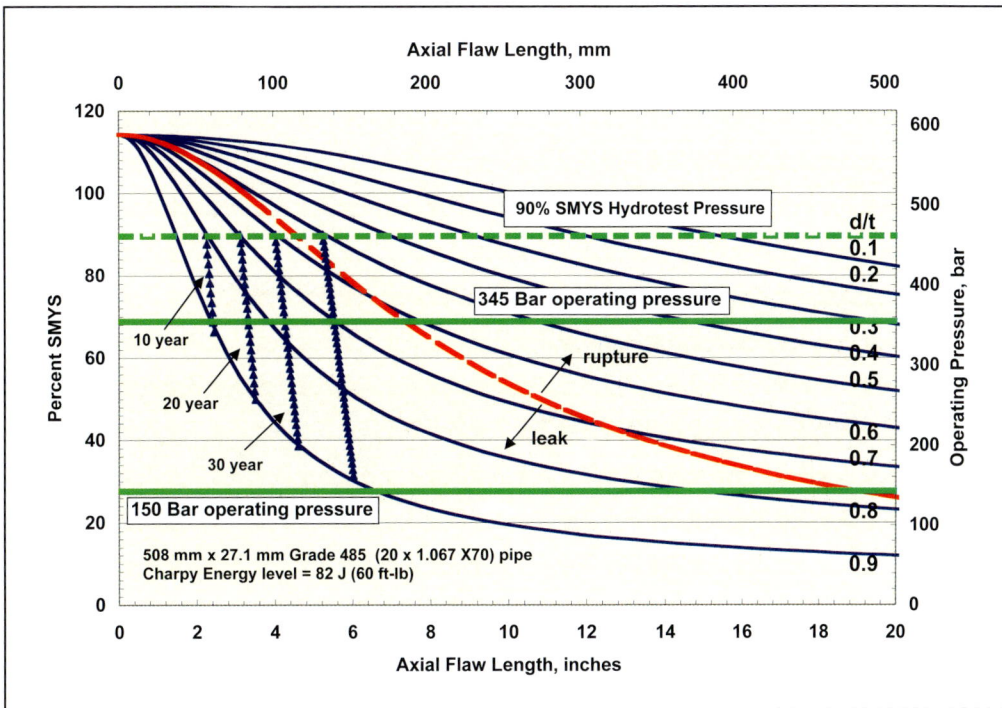

FIGURE 7. PIPE FAILURE HOOP STRESS VS. CORROSION FLAW SIZE – EXTERNAL CORROSION RATE OF 0.254 MM/YR (0.0098 INCH/YR)

From this figure it should be concluded with a high degree of confidence that external corrosion would not be a primary risk of concern for this pipeline. This observation assumes that the appropriate cathodic protection is made operational in a timely manner, and close interval surveys are properly undertaken to ensure no external selective corrosion "hot spots," where external corrosion rate could be accelerated, develop over the life of the pipeline. Close interval surveys employ various above ground inspection techniques to periodically determine the effectiveness of the CP system and pipeline coating to resist external corrosion on a pipeline.

Gas Velocity and Pipe Erosion

The actual gas velocity within a production pipeline is critical for two reasons: erosion velocity and liquid loading. Erosion can occur because of high velocities within the pipeline especially from gas associated with production wells that can contain solids such as sand. Velocity changes can also place additional load stresses on a pipeline from liquid slugging as liquid that is dropped out at lower flow rates is swept back up when gas flow is increased, causing changes in mass flow or "slugs." Actual gas velocity is dependent on pressure. The higher the pressure, the lower the actual gas velocity within the pipe for the same design mass flow rate. At the design capacity and pressure ranges stated for this pipeline we do not see any critical concerns related to internal erosion, as actual flow velocities should be well below erosion thresholds.[10]

Abnormal Loading Issues

Paramount for the pipeline operator is the requirement to determine, calculate, and document solutions for all abnormal loading conditions, both internal (slugging, temperature change, etc.) and external (e.g., crush, earth movement such as landslide, etc.) that the pipeline might experience. While we would expect a thick-walled pipeline to absorb some limited earth movement, we find very disturbing comments suggesting that a serious landslide can be

---

[10] Maximum flow of pipeline from Figure 2 is 350 MMSCF/D, and using a pressure range of approximately 100 to 345 Bar.

absorbed by this pipeline without failure.[11] Detailed loading calculations for major land movement developed by the pipeline operator need to be carefully scrutinized as the author knows of no pipeline that can take high mass, high momentum external loading associated with large landslides. Figure 8 speaks volumes for the kinds of land mass flow that can be expected in the area. The author understands that a pipeline route that places the pipe above the landslide might leave the pipe suspended and thick-walled pipe should be able to take some extreme "left hanging" loading forces. However, any suggestions that the pipeline should be routed either at the base of such landmass, or within the major flow of potential land movement needs to be seriously challenged and reviewed. Failure of the pipe in these severe loading conditions, in all probability, will result in full bore ruptures. There are methods to protect pipelines in such high-risk land movement areas, but no mention is made in any public documents of these approaches. In such higher risk land movement areas, a prudent pipeline operator may endeavor

FIGURE 8. AREA LANDSLIDES

to reroute the pipeline out of the area, removing the risk. He could also elect to bury the pipe deep into stable bedrock or soil, or otherwise shelter the pipe, from the unstable soil. Reroute is preferred as it is usually the most effective approach.

Peat, a unique form of boggy acidic soil, is a special type of environment that can place abnormal loads on the pipeline from movement, especially as the design of this pipeline is negatively buoyant, wanting to sink within the peat. The operator has indicated that the pipeline will traverse these peat conditions by spanning the pipeline along stone column supports within peat bogs. The designers should be able to demonstrate through clear documentation and calculations that a particular pipeline route, design, and span through peat will not generate abnormal loading on the pipe that can cause its failure.

Pipeline Safety Equipment

In the design of pipeline safety systems, there can be a tendency to stay on one course based on an original "game plan" while attempting to correct serious deficiencies by incorporating additional changes to "fix" the original flawed design premise. The very nature of these "fixes" introduces complexity that can inadvertently drive the system to the very failure needing to be avoided. In complex energy system design such as high-pressure pipelines, we call this phenomenon of adding complexity to fix simple fundamental basic design premise errors, "Space Shuttle Syndrome." This label was coined after the NASA Challenger space shuttle loss and verified again after the second Columbia shuttle loss, and subsequently reaffirmed in the July, 2005 Discovery space shuttle launch. In Discovery's case, after approximately two billion dollars and a two year engineering effort, the foam hitting the shuttle on launch, the same problem that caused the Columbia's loss, had all too obviously not been fixed. Space Shuttle Syndrome has come to mean a complex organisation rushing to launch at all costs,

Is the Corrib project another space shuttle rushing to launch at all costs without listening to reason about a flawed initial design or routing approach?

failing to fix or address fundamentally flawed initial approaches, while utilising poor risk management to cloak their misguided confidence that everything will work.

---

[11] Corrib Field Development Project, "Onshore Pipeline Quantified Risk Assessment," Version F, dated April 22, 2005.

It has been stated that the onshore Corrib Pipeline will be failsafe. This term has been getting much misuse in the industry, especially with regard to its application in poor risk analysis. As defined by this author for this pipeline, failsafe is the design philosophy such that failure of a component or operator mis-operation cannot place the pipeline in an overpressure event that could result in pipe failure. As demonstrated in Figures 5 and 7, at these exotic pressures the room for error on the onshore pipeline is very small. We find it incredible that, given these very high pressures, more documentation has not been presented to clearly instill confidence that the onshore pipeline pressures will be maintained in the pressure ranges suggested by the operator.

For example, the wise addition of an onshore remote operated valve will reduce the outrageously long depressurising time (many hours) associated with an onshore pipeline rupture as the many kilometres of offshore system depressurising out the failure site will continue should this valve not be quickly closed. Incredibly, this remote valve was apparently not in the original design scheme suggesting a serious lack of appreciation of gas pipeline dynamics and failure consequences by the decision team. This remote valve (even if it were designed to automatically close), however, will not really impact the consequences associated with leaks or ruptures on the onshore pipeline. For leaks, the gas inventory is so large that the leak will in all probability result in an incident before the line can be depressurised. In a pipeline rupture, most consequences (i.e., fatalities) will occur in the early minutes of the rupture and the valve's closure will not occur in sufficient time to avoid a catastrophe from this highly compressed fluid. The valve on the boundary of the onshore pipeline is not really a true "safety" in the event of an onshore pipeline failure, though it will reduce the number of minutes that an onshore rupture could blow down out the pipeline. As will be shown in Section IV Onshore Pipeline Routing Issues, reducing the blow down time from a rupture to minutes will still result in very large fatality zones.

The Difference Between Base Design and Future Operation

While on the subject of the onshore valve, there have been varying statements about what the maximum pressures will really be for the onshore pipeline. If the operator cannot adequately demonstrate that the onshore pipeline will be truly "failsafe" (e.g., protected to prevent pressures in excess of 150 Bar, approximately 30 % SMYS), this pipeline needs to be moved and rerouted away from population.

We need to be very clear in keeping with the above system complexity comments that a pressure letdown control device designed to drop pressure at the shoreline will not be a failsafe design. Such a control would most likely introduce other system complexities that would substantially increase the likelihood of an onshore pipeline failure.

No credible design scheme has been provided that commits or ensures that onshore pipeline pressures will remain below 150 Bar.

In any pipeline system one must have a clear understanding of and commitment to the basic system design to prevent overpressure. Relying on flowing (or dynamic) pressure drop to maintain safe operating pressure ranges represents poor engineering and management practices that should not be obscured by QRA attempts. Future pressure limitation commitments go with the design routing of the pipeline, as the current base design does not restrict the pipeline operating pressure in the future. For example, the entire onshore Corrib pipeline will be tested to permit a pressure of 345 Bar. There is no restriction on the pipeline operator to maintain or restrict future operating pressure so the operator could exceed 150 Bar and even reach the 345 Bar limit. The pipeline operator is not required to recertify the integrity of the pipeline or even notify the public before increasing to exotic higher pressures should he decide to increase the onshore pipeline pressure for whatever reason. A brief review of Figures 5 and 7 would clearly reinforce the real risks associated with the pressure ranges between 150 and 345 Bar for this system. The rupture flow dynamics and associated large fatality zones discussed in the next section, will help one gain an appreciation of the importance of avoiding rupture on this unique system at these exotically high pressures.

IV. Onshore Pipeline Routing Issues

Proximity to Population

One major factor when determining the route for a new on land pipeline is its proximity to population, usually captured as dwellings and unsheltered gathering areas (schoolyards or soccer fields for example). Depending on a country's standards or regulations, there may be minimum distance requirements that set or influence some of the choices for a pipeline's route. Various countries set no minimum distances between structures, unsheltered gathering sites, and pipelines, while others do.

BS 8010 attempts to address some of the concerns associated with population in proximity to pipelines using a classification of location designation that sets a design factor. There is a major weakness in setting the design factor for a pipeline via classification of location approach based on a population density approach of so many people per hectare. [12] Population density determinations don't adequately address the issue where a pipeline may elect to come in close to concentrations of people in sparsely populated countryside, that still meet the lower density requirement for location of class 1, such as small towns. A class 1 location permits pipelines to operate up to 72% SMYS (for this pipeline this factor places pressures in serious pipeline rupture territory). To help address the shortcoming of population density in class location approaches, BS 8010 to its credit also sets for methane (in Figure 2 chart within Part 2 of the standard) a minimum distance requirement for normally occupied buildings. Unfortunately, this chart only reflects pipeline pressures up to 100 Bar. The current proposed pipeline route through Rossport and other nearby villages meets the lowest population density class 1 location, but the pipeline pressures are off the chart and dwellings are close to the proposed pipeline route. BS 8010 allows pipelines off the chart provided a risk analysis meeting certain requirements is performed. A review of the proposed onshore pipeline route indicated in Figure 3, highlighting dwellings in close proximity to the pipeline, should underscore the problem and the reason for so much past effort being directed to risk assessments for this pipeline (the closest dwelling is apparently 70 metres from the pipeline).

Understanding Pipeline Releases

When discussing high pressure gas pipeline releases, it is important for the reader to understand the two release scenarios associated with the discharge of highly compressed gas, leaks and ruptures. At pressures greater than approximately 1 Bar, gas pipeline release will discharge at the speed of sound. This phenomenon, also commonly known as choked flow, is a property of the ratio of the heat capacities and the temperature of the gas.[13] For most natural gas rich streams and temperatures, the speed of sound is approximately 300 to 430 metres/sec (1000 to 1400 ft/sec) depending on how one compensates for non-ideal gas factors associated with highly turbulent high velocity flows. Regardless of the hole size, whether a pinhole leak or a full bore pipe rupture, the velocity of the gas will usually be limited by the speed of sound at the hole conditions. The major difference between a leak and a rupture, other than the fracture dynamics described earlier, is the difference in mass flow rate.

Mass flow rate determinations for leaks can be fairly easily calculated by assuming an orifice hole size and estimating the pipeline pressure (which stays essentially constant at the leak location). Leaks can be very destructive if the gas can become capped or trapped in structures where it can then accumulate (leading to higher probability of building explosions). At the higher operating pressures of this pipeline, leaks can still release a great deal of gas.

---

[12] The design factor sets the maximum permitted percent of SMYS, or "internal design pressure," that has a specific meaning in the BS 8010 standard. The lower the design factor the lower the permitted maximum pressure.
[13] Gas composition will change the ratio of the heat capacities for a gas mixture.

Full bore ruptures release considerably larger mass at much higher rates than leaks. For rupture, the mass flow release rapidly spikes upward and then starts to decay with time. Mass release is defined by the full bore orifice (combined rate from the two open ends of the pipeline) and upstream/downstream gas pressures that will not drop quickly on a high-pressure gas pipeline. The mass flow changes with time as the density of the gas, not the velocity, changes with time. These density changes are a function of various factors associated with a particular pipeline. This concept is difficult for the layman and many engineers to understand, but pipeline ruptures are not like a balloon bursting where loss of containment drops pressure to atmospheric almost instantaneously.

The nature of a rupture mass release spike, or increase, and its subsequent decline depends on pipeline size, pressure, pipe hydraulics, pipeline length, deviation from ideal gas and, most importantly, the time to recognise and change the main gas flow near the rupture (time to recognise and actually close nearby valves if any are available). Dynamic simulation tools are used to predict mass releases over time for ruptures at specific locations on a specific pipeline. Depending on many complexities, there is a tendency for too many engineers to believe these models calculate exact releases. In reality, they are far from exact, especially when their efforts fail to properly capture the poor recognition times associated with remotely identifying a pipeline rupture. This delay adds greatly to already high mass release estimates, especially in the critical early stages of a rupture where fatalities are most likely to occur because of high mass releases with ignition (which usually occurs within minutes if not seconds).

It is easy for inexperienced engineers to believe that their calculations modeling a pipeline rupture at a specific point are exact, when in reality many transients can easily modify such calculated results by a wide margin. Two major and serious deficiencies we find in risk management approaches concerning pipeline ruptures are assumptions: 1) that rupture modeling assumes instantaneous or almost instantaneous identification by the SCADA or remote monitoring system of a rupture, and rapid (nearby) valve closure, and 2) that the massive air/fuel mixture doesn't explode or ignite quickly. Neither one of these assumptions is realistic especially for those very high pressures that can create their own ignition. Such erroneous assumptions critically understate the fatality zones and risks associated with a high-pressure gas pipeline rupture as will be explained in the next two sections.

A Reality Check on Understanding Gas Pipeline Ruptures

Given the incomplete information provided in previous public documents describing the dynamics and thermal consequence zones associated with a Corrib pipeline rupture, this author believes additional detail about this failure consequence is warranted. As clearly demonstrated in Figures 5 and 7, thick-walled pipe is far from invincible to failure, either as a leak or a rupture. Specifically focusing on ruptures, Figure 9 should serve as a reality check for anyone calculating or attempting to model gas pipeline rupture impact zones for regulatory or standard development, or for siting of high pressure gas pipelines.

Figure 9 is a photo of the Carlsbad, New Mexico, August 19, 2000 natural gas transmission pipeline rupture. This pipeline was a 30-inch pipeline with a 0.335 inch (8.51 mm) wall thickness (thin-walled pipe), Grade X-52 (52,000 psi SMYS), operating at a pressure of 675 psig (46.6 Barg) that failed from internal corrosion.[14] By now Figures 5 and 7 should have dispensed with any illusions that thick-walled and thin-walled pipe at these high stress level operating pressures will somehow fail differently.

---

[14] NTSB Pipeline Accident Report, "Natural Gas Pipeline Rupture and Fire Near Carlsbad, New Mexico August 19, 2000," NTSB/PAR-03/01, Adopted February 11, 2003.

FIGURE 9. CARLSBAD, NEW MEXICO NATURAL GAS TRANSMISSION PIPELINE RUPTURE (COURTESY OF THE NTSB)

To gain an appreciation of the height of the flame in Figure 9, the steel support towers are 24 metres (80 feet) tall which would place the flame at almost 110 meters (370 ft) into the air. Given the time needed to get a camera to the site to take this picture (the flame burned for approximately 55 minutes) it would be fair to assume that the photo was taken some time after the pipe rupture so the fuel release represented in the photo is well below the peak rapid spike increased mass flow which occurs at initial failure.

Figure 10 is an aerial photo of the Carlsbad failure site taken in the aftermath that should help everyone gain an appreciation of the thermal impact zone associated with a pipeline rupture. The nearest steel pipe support suspension tower on the river's edge is approximately 183 meters (600 ft) from the rupture site. An extended family of 12 (including five children) camping approximately 206 meters (675 ft) from the ruptured pipe all died as a result of the blast and thermal radiation received. Six of the victims, even though they were able to run and jump into the river further away from the failure and in the shadow of the river gully, still received fatal thermal dosages and (given the extent of 3rd degree burns over their bodies) died within hours. I do not provide these photos to scare or unduly alarm anyone, but rather to call serious attention to the fact that engineers and risk managers sometimes forget that the numbers they are oftentimes overworking fail to match the reality, especially if they are mistaken in their critical assumptions. Carlsbad serves as a very real reality check for anyone making poor risk management pipeline decisions.

Referring to Figure 10, one can get an appreciation of how rupture events extend well beyond the pipeline right of way. Once ignited, the large flame height significantly increases the thermal radiation dosage zone of the burning cloud. In the Carlsbad event, the steel towers were thermally stressed so badly that they and the pipelines they supported across the river had to be removed from service.

FIGURE 10. CARLSBAD PIPELINE RUPTURE, THE AFTERMATH (COURTESY OF THE NTSB)

Because the phenomenon of gas jetting, roaring or blowing directly out the end of a pipeline rupture, is often misrepresented in risk analysis to understate impact zones or risk, further discussion is needed on this important issue. All buried gas pipeline ruptures gas jet and very few generate flames that hug the ground. In fact, Figure 9 represents a flame from a gas jetting failure. Eventually, upon ignition, all the impact energy is dissipated and thermal energy raises the flame off the ground extending the impact zones. A closer examination of Figure 10 will indicate the typical circle of thermal impact zone from a rupture flame. In this case the photo doesn't extend beyond the service bridge, but the thermal burn zone (described in the NTSB report narrative) extended well beyond the service bridge and across the river, an area approximately 423 m (1400 ft) from the rupture site. The NTSB report clearly indicates that pipeline emergency response personnel were not able to cross the service bridge with vehicles to get to a nearby valve because of the high thermal flux. The point to be made here is that gas jetting doesn't really reduce the radius for the thermal impact zone, it just moves the thermal zone circle down the pipeline and the zone can extend well beyond any right-of-way. Note the relative absence of extended severe thermal burning in the opposite direction of the towers upstream of the rupture crater site (toward top of the photo).

Finally, to put to rest any illusions that a gas jetting at sonic velocity from a pipeline rupture may be an insignificant event, Figure 11 is another photo of the crater from the Carlsbad release.

This photo is looking downstream of the rupture toward the river (the bottom of Figure 10). The crater in this rupture case was only approximately 34 m long by 16 m wide (113 ft long by 51 ft wide). The pipe missing between the arrows was shrapneled in several pieces many hundreds of feet from the crater

FIGURE 11. CARLSBAD RUPTURE CRATER (COURTESY OF NTSB)

(part of the fracture process as the pipe fails in microseconds). The author has taken particular time to benchmark the Carlsbad rupture because of the extensive clear documentation on this specific failure, including time to ignition that permits a reality check for those utilising various pipeline rupture models. The author must state for the record that the Carlsbad pipeline failure is considered a moderate mass flow release for a high-pressure gas pipeline rupture. A Corrib Pipeline rupture, even though it is a smaller diameter pipeline, will release much more fuel at a higher rate during the early critical minutes of a pipeline failure where ignition and subsequent fatalities are most likely (as will be described shortly).

> A Corrib onshore pipeline rupture in Rossport above 150 bar pressure will release fuel at a much higher rate in the early critical fatality minutes, and in all probability generate a much bigger flame than that shown in Figure 9 for the Carlsbad tragedy.

Despite previous claims in some Corrib pipeline documents inferring that natural gas pipeline ruptures don't ignite, much less explode, the author invites the reader to review the website analysing the various explosions and blast forces determined for the Carlsbad event recorded on distant seismographs.

The New Mexico Pipeline Explosion Seismic Signals site where this information may be reviewed is:

http://www.ees.nmt.edu/Geop/Pipeline/pipeline.html

From these seismic measurements, time to ignition after pipe rupture at Carlsbad was determined to be approximately 24 seconds. Contrary to previous opinions stated in Corrib pipeline public documents, pipeline ruptures do not need a flame source to ignite a very large and turbulent gas cloud. Despite the fairly tight flammability range of natural gas (5 to 15 vol.%), many gas pipeline ruptures ignite for various reasons. Sparks generated by pipe shrapnel, thrown rocks sparking, and static electricity are just a few of the sources of ignition in addition to flame sources. For these massive rate releases, ignition usually occurs in the early minutes of release when mass flow has spiked at its highest and is starting its decay, but is still very large.

Corrib Pipeline Rupture Impact Zone

Figures 12 and 13 indicate energy release or thermal flux (in KW/m^2) as a function of distance from the pipeline for the Corrib onshore pipeline estimated for the boundary condition pressures of 150 Bar and 345 Bar, respectively. The two graphs represent a full-bore rupture release, corrected for non ideal gas effects associated with high flow turbulence, occurring in the vicinity of the neighboring Rossport homes. An instantaneous ignition curve (t= 0 seconds) and delayed ignition at various other times have also been estimated for reference. The thermal flux curves declining as a function of distance is characteristic of any major flame source from a pipeline rupture. The thermal flux decay with time is representative of mass flow degradation from high pressure pipelines. The spread between the time to ignition curves will be a function of pipeline hydraulics, point of rupture, the compressed gas inventory (e.g., density), and response time to close nearby valves.

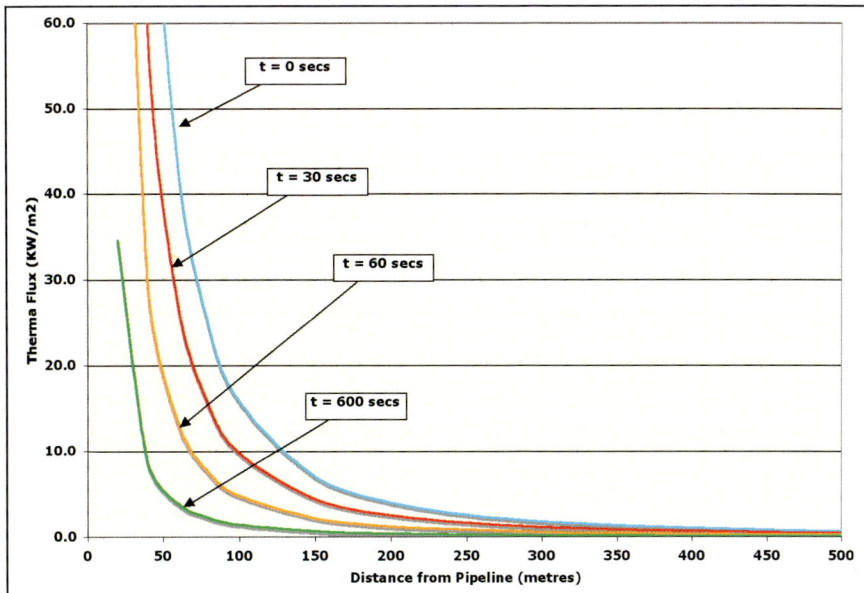

FIGURE 12. CORRIB ONSHORE PIPELINE RUPTURE THERMAL FLUX VS. DISTANCE FROM PIPELINE 150 BAR CASE

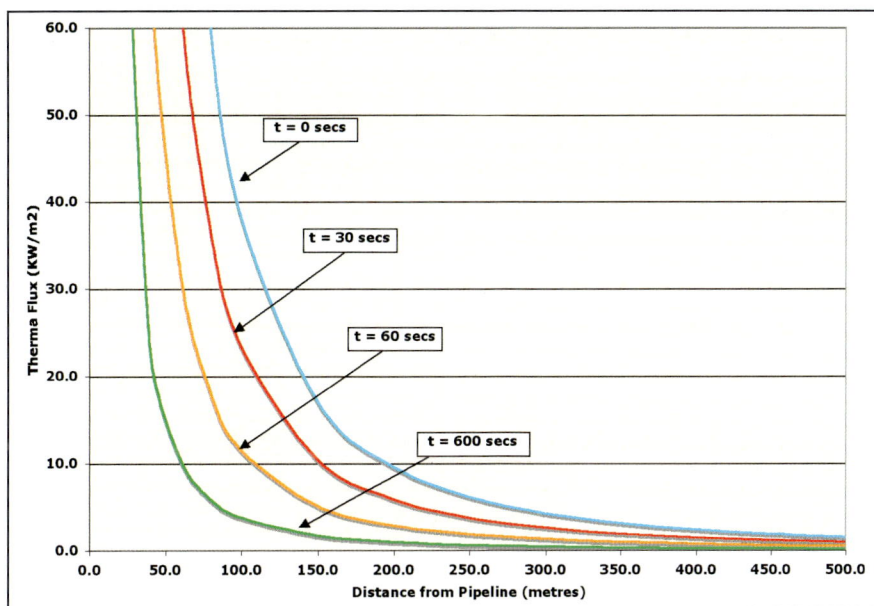

FIGURE 13. CORRIB ONSHORE PIPELINE RUPTURE THERMAL FLUX VS. DISTANCE FROM PIPELINE 345 BAR CASE

Unlike some thermal release curves developed for pipeline ruptures that run out for many minutes, and as a result downplay or miss the very high flux "thermal load" band, we have focused the thermal release graphs to draw attention to the early minutes (the first ten minutes) of a pipeline rupture. This is the most likely time for ignition/explosion (usually within 1 or 2 minutes) with high thermal fluxes and thermal loads most associated with fatalities. Depending on what transients and assumptions are utilized in any dynamic model, the results may be slightly different, but the general shape, approximate time to decay and high heat fluxes, will be characteristic for an onshore rupture on this system. The critical determination of the fatality zone will be the probability call for time to ignition. Note that the higher heat flux associated

21

with 345 Bar is representative of a mass release more than twice the rate associated with the 150 Bar case.

Given the release forces associated with very high pressure pipelines and the large associated fatality zones, the burden of proof should fall on the operator to demonstrate why ignition will not occur, especially in the early moments of release that can result in the greatest risks of fatalities. At these high pressures, prudent modeling should assume essentially instantaneous ignition when determining pipeline routing near people.

Figures 12 and 13 only tell part of the overall equation as the thermal flux for a certain distance needs to be translated (estimated from Figures 12 or 13) into a thermal dosage that either causes serious burns, fatality, or dwelling loss. Figure 14 represents a series of thermal dosage models derived from industry accepted thermal models.[15] Figure 14 is a "time to" chart graphically illustrating the time to which a fixed thermal flux can be tolerated for unsheltered

> Pipeline rupture siting analysis must incorporate the early minutes of initial ignition when causalities from high heat flux are at their greatest.

(exposed) individuals and wooden structures. For example, a 20 KW/m^2 heat flux exposure for only a few seconds will result in 1 % mortality for those caught outside near a rupture, while a few seconds later at this thermal flux, 50 % mortality will result, and in slightly over one minute 100 % mortality of unsheltered individuals will result. A wooden structure receiving the same heat flux of 20 KW/m^2 should be able to survive, as this flux is left of the wooden dwelling spontaneous ignition curve drawn indicating that essentially, a wooden structure can take this heat flux indefinitely. Depending on the accuracy of the thermal model, Figure 13 would suggest that a dwelling approximately 150 metres from the pipeline would not "spontaneously ignite." This does not mean that secondary effects won't occur (i.e., vehicles explode).

Focusing on dwellings, however does not tell the full story. Often in risk analysis, assumptions are made that individuals caught outside in close proximity to a pipeline rupture will have the presence of mind to run and seek shelter from the heat. As figure 14 clearly illustrates, the time

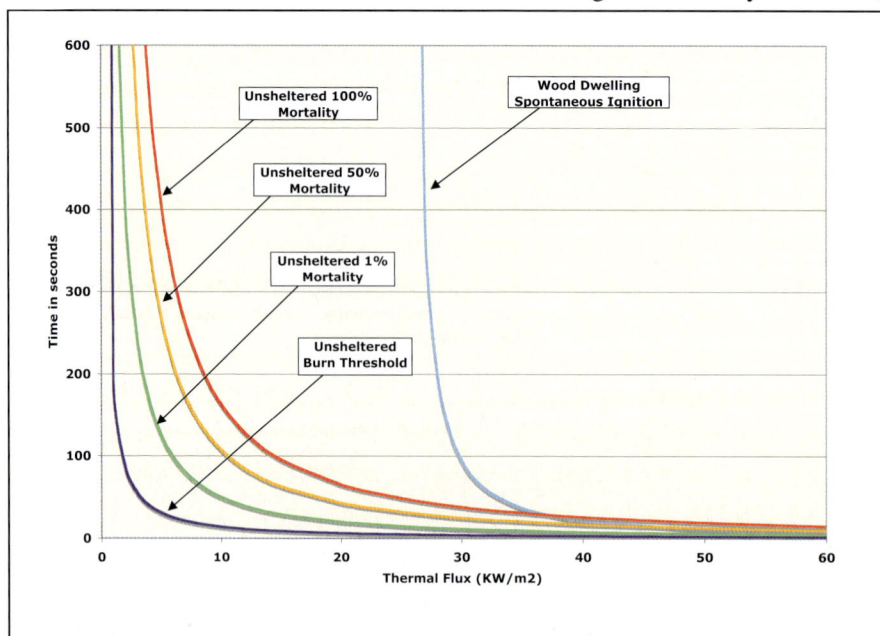

FIGURE 14. "TIME TO" FOR VARIOUS THERMAL FLUXES ON PEOPLE AND WOODEN STRUCTURES

---

[15] Various thermal dosage models quoted from GRI, " A Model for Sizing High Consequence Areas Associated with Natural Gas Pipelines," prepared by C-FER Technologies, October 2000.

to get into a shelter, away from the heat is measured in seconds. Figure 14 would also suggest that a 5 KW/m^2 heat flux provides only minutes for people to leave the area if they can. At 5 KW/m^2 heat flux, individuals within 300 metres of the pipeline are at risk. The Carlsbad reality check would, however, suggests that a more appropriate buffer zone for unsheltered individuals is 400 to 500 metres, and 200 metres for dwellings.

BS 8010's graph to 100 bars pressure is definitely coming up short on dwelling survival distance, but in all fairness the standard probably didn't envision such high pressure pipelines, as in the Corrib proposal, that can generate large heat fluxes for many minutes. These are large distance numbers, but again these are exotically high pressures, which begs the question "Who would want to run such a high pressure pipeline near people, especially when there appear to be many more remote routing options?" More restrictive countries establish lower

> Early ignition scenarios and Carlsbad would place the safe distance for a dwelling at 200 metres and the safe distances for unsheltered individuals beyond 400 metres.

KW/m^2 values as an offsite acceptable heat flux for facilities that can generate high thermal flux, while less progressive countries have higher threshold values, or none at all, for pipeline events.[16]

For those who may argue that someone located outside can run away from a pipeline flame and thus decrease the suggested safety zone, running will not compensate for the very high initial thermal load (radiation dosage) that can and will most likely occur on rupture. At these high thermal loads, credit for running to a safe distance is inappropriate. Imagine trying to maintain a frame of mind while running with your clothes and skin on fire! Referring back to Figure 10, the unfortunate victims in the Carlsbad tragedy, even if they had reached and crossed the service bridge, had already received and were continuing to receive fatal thermal dosages from the very high early thermal flux. In the Carlsbad case, no matter what direction and how fast the individuals had run, they were well beyond (right of) the "Time to" curve for 100 % mortality exposure shown in Figure 14 because of the severe initial thermal loading associated with early ignition. It is a mistake to portray that such high thermal loading occurs on high pressure gas pipeline system ruptures only for a few seconds.

---

[16] The U.S. has no defined federal pipeline siting regulations and no acceptable thermal flux limit for pipeline ruptures, though a 15.8 KW/m^2 (5000 BTU/hr ft^2) is often implied in analysis wrongfully suggesting there are such requirements to justify poor pipeline route selection.

FIGURE 15. ROSSPORT 400 METRE RUPTURE IMPACT ZONE

The green band lines in Figure 15 represent an approximate 400 metre zone from the proposed pipeline in proximity to Rossport. Most of the citizens are within the band for unsheltered individuals. Note the large number of dwellings in close proximity to the pipeline well within 200 metres from the pipeline.

Sensitive Waterways

When reviewing possible routes for pipelines, priority is usually given to routes that avoid people as demonstrated by the discussion in the previous section. As possible routes are evaluated, additional environmental restrictions may come into play influencing route alternatives. Depending on a country's regulatory environment, these restrictions usually manifest themselves as conditions pertaining to sensitive waterways containing susceptible ecosystems.

It is the nature of gas systems that their failure is less prone to permanently damage large ecosystems. There will be exceptions to this statement, but it is generally true. Ironically, for a gas pipeline system, most of the ecological damage or risk from such damage usually occurs in the construction phase. Pipeline construction teams can get ahead of the operator's best intentions, especially if project schedules are pressing (as they usually always are).

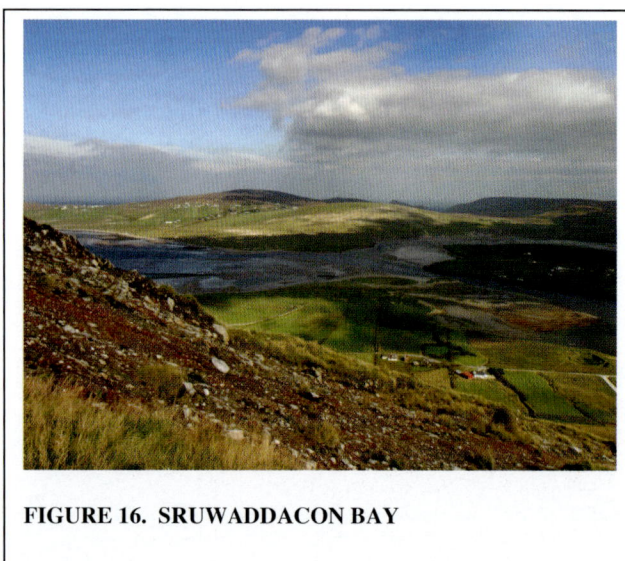

FIGURE 16. SRUWADDACON BAY

In first reviewing the proposed onshore pipeline route, this author was struck with the question of why is the land route in close proximity to so many people?

It is this author's opinion that the current proposed land route has more to do with ease of construction and shortest pipeline path (cheapest route mentality) than a properly evaluated route selection. Given this author's experience and background, and a natural bias to first focus on protecting people, the next observation was why didn't the operator consider a route up the middle of the Sruwaddacon Bay? Closer examination suggests that a bay route does not provide quite enough proximity distance. It also appears that the bay may be a sensitive route with some very unusual construction and tidal surge challenges. This author has difficulty accepting the premise that all the other options for possible pipeline landfall are so difficult or restrictive so as to leave only the general bay location scheme.

A further analysis of pipeline route alternatives is warranted to ensure that options were properly reviewed and analysed should an onshore gas plant prove acceptable.

V. Pipeline Construction Issues

The pipeline is to be constructed to DNV OS-F101 SAWL standards, which is claimed to be equivalent to API 5L grade X 70. The pipe will have a nominal outside diameter of 508mm (20 inches) with a nominal thickness of 27.1 mm (1.07 inch). This is considered thick-walled pipe.

The Thick-Walled Pipe Conundrum

Thick-walled pipe brings certain positive benefits and certain different concerns. For example, thick-walled pipe operating at high stress levels increase the likelihood of third party damage becoming a time dependent failure.[17] It is important to realize that, in many cases, the thicker the pipe the greater the safety margin. This safety benefit, however, rapidly diminishes as the operating pressure as a percentage of SMYS increases. As mentioned and demonstrated in detail (see Figures 5 and 7), thick-walled pipe is not invincible to various failure threats such as corrosion that can cause either leak or rupture releases. Any attempts to represent that thick-walled pipe is invincible or that it can be treated with disrespect needs to be seriously challenged, as modern pipe fracture mechanics will prove such perspectives most unwise.

Thick-walled pipe also presents difficulties for smart pig or inline inspection (ILI) as discussed in detail in Section VI Operational and Maintenance Issues of Concern. Certain smart pig inspection technologies will not work well on thick-walled pipe, a point that has not been mentioned in previous Corrib pipeline public documents, implying that ILI will be a highly effective safety net on this system. Given the importance that corrosion, especially internal corrosion can play on possible premature pipe failure, specific information related to ILI inspection claims and performance need to be clearly defined and documented. Over reliance on ILI performance or effectiveness in a risk analysis to prevent pipe failure from corrosion could prove fatal with this pipeline. New ILI inspection processes have recently been promulgated as an API industry standard to better define the limits of ILI applications on a specific pipeline; a much needed improvement for the pipeline industry that may utilise ILI as an integrity management tool.[18]

---

[17] It is a very serious mischaracterisation for any risk analysis to utilise historical databases in their statistics suggesting the same third party damage frequencies on pipelines (even thick-walled) that are operating at much lower stress levels.

[18] American Petroleum Institute, API Standard 1163, "In-line Inspection Systems Qualification Standard, "First Edition, August, 2005.

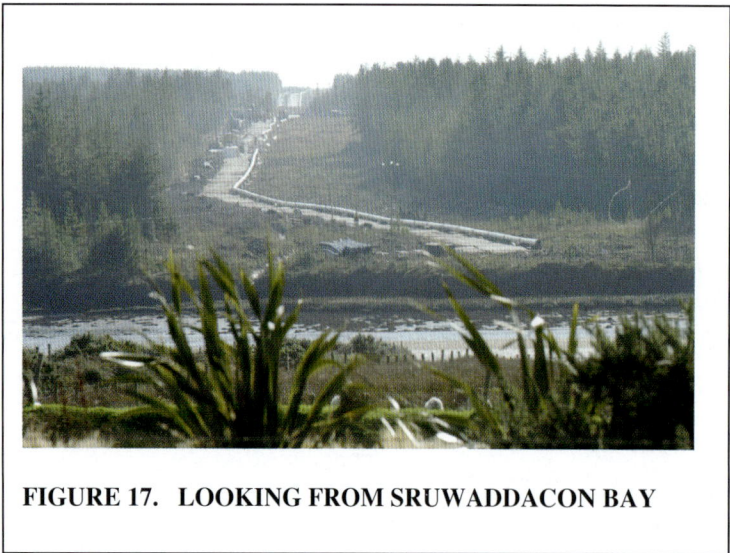

FIGURE 17. LOOKING FROM SRUWADDACON BAY

Girth Weld Inspection and Integrity Testing

One example of the problems that can be associated with thick-walled pipe is the importance of properly inspecting all girth welds joining pipe segments. Conventional x-ray radiography is ineffective at penetrating or clearly indicating thick welds. Usually ultrasonic technology is utilised for such pipe. We strongly advise that all records of onshore pipeline weld inspection be cataloged, auditable by an independent third party inspection organisation, and maintained for the life of this pipeline, wherever it is routed. This is especially important given the potential abnormal loading stresses associated with earth movement that the pipeline may face, as discussed previously, that may place additional stress on the girth welds. To be very clear, the initial high-pressure hydrotest (certifying the pipeline to operate at stress levels up to 72% SMYS) does not adequately or sufficiently test the girth welds on a pipeline that is going to see potential abnormal loading conditions. It is very important to clearly understand that a hydrotest test will not adequately test girth welds and that a girth weld failure will manifest itself as a pipeline rupture. At the potentially exotic pressures that this pipeline could see, there is little room or margin for error.

VI. Operational and Maintenance Issues of Concern

Corrosion Monitoring Program

There should be considerable concern raised on any gas production pipeline operating at these pressures and relying solely on corrosion inhibitor and corrosion monitoring, utilising only corrosion coupons. A reading of the previously cited NTSB Carlsbad pipeline failure report should demonstrate the shortcomings of overly relying on corrosion coupons.[19]   The shortcomings of such programs are well documented.[20]   Over reliance on corrosion coupons to monitor internal corrosion should be taken as a warning sign that internal corrosion may be not under control, a serious risk of failure for this very unique system. The cited reference standard for this pipeline, BS 8010, section 4.3, discusses application of corrosion inhibitor and corrosion coupons.[21]   We would characterise this standard as deficient or incomplete in this area, especially given the importance that internal corrosion can play on production pipelines as demonstrated by Figure 5, even for thick-walled pipe.

The operator has asserted that the subsea design of this system makes application of an important component of an effective internal corrosion prevention program, a proper cleaning pig program (such as a sphere), unattainable.[22]   The failure to incorporate a prudent cleaning pig program, especially for the onshore pipeline, should raise concerns about the ability of the operator to adequately prevent selective internal corrosion on this pipeline. A competent corrosion cleaning pigging program extends well beyond just running the cleaning pig.

---

[19] Ibid., NTSB Carlsbad Incident Report.

[20] Richard B.Kuprewicz, "Preventing Pipeline Releases," Prepared for the Washington City County Pipeline Safety Consortium, July 22, 2003.

[21] Ibid., BS 8010 1992 version.

[22] An Bord Pleanála, "Inspector's Report on Gas Terminal at Bellagelly South, Bellanaboy Bridge, Belmullet, Co. Mayo," signed by Kevin Moore and dated April, 2003.

26

Analysis of material removed with the pig, especially for corrosion products, is important to identify internal corrosion activity at possible "hotspots" that the inhibitor may not prevent, or coupons not indicate. This could lead to premature failure. The importance of properly evaluating internal corrosion rate in any analysis on this pipeline should be evident from a review of Figures 4 and 5 as selective corrosion can seriously reduce the integrity of this pipeline. Assuming there is no internal corrosion because one's corrosion inhibitor program and coupon monitoring program is assumed to work is a delusion fraught with much danger, especially given the proposed routing of this pipeline.

Smart Pigging and Thick-Walled Pipe

Smart pigging or inline inspection (ILI) is often claimed to be the superior method of inspecting pipelines for certain flaws or anomalies that can lead to failure, either leak or rupture. What is not well understood is that misapplication of the smart pigging process, such as the choice of the wrong pig, and mismanagement of the pig determinations and verifications can seriously render ILI ineffective.[23] New industry standards have now been incorporated to address some of these serious shortcomings concerning the misapplication of ILI to confirm pipeline integrity.[24] We find the public documents published to date for the Corrib pipeline to be incomplete and seriously deficient in detail concerning the issues of ILI and thick-walled pipe reliable inspection. Given the importance that ILI can play in preventing failure from corrosion, any risk analysis that fails to properly address ILI effectiveness on this system would be deemed critically deficient.

The application of smart pigging on thick-walled pipelines is not without serious challenges. The implication that such tools will prevent failure are overstated, a definite risk when taken in combination with other missing elements of an effective corrosion program. No details are provided about which ILI smart pig technology will be utilised to inspect this pipeline, a serious deficiency in any risk analysis approach. In all probability more than one smart pig technology will be required as running only one type of ILI is usually considered an indication of an incomplete ILI program. There are at least two serious threats that require different smart pig technologies, corrosion and third party damage of the type discussed shortly, which can result in time dependent pipe failure. There is a serious probability that QRAs to date have overstated the effectiveness of these important programs to prevent failure on this pipeline, and understated the likelihood of failure as a result.

> Running a smart pig is the easiest and usually cheapest part of an overall effective ILI inspection program. Much more effort is involved in choosing the right pig and verifying and responding to pig observations.

Third Party Damage Concerns

While it is usually true that the thicker the pipe the higher the potential to avoid failure in many cases, this statement must be taken in the context of operating pressure, specifically the much higher likelihood that this pipeline will be operated at very high stress levels as mentioned previously. While thicker pipe tends to resist or prevent immediate failure from third party damage, this damage (i.e., cuts, gouges, grooves) is subject to cycling growth-induced failure at a later date. For the high stress levels expected on this production pipeline, we find risk analysis indicating that thick pipe will not be subject to cycle induced fatigue failure and thus "not a risk of concern" to be inadequate.

> Risk analysis conclusions dismissing fatigue cycle induced third party damage failure on this high stress level pipeline appear incomplete.

[23] Richard B. Kuprewicz, "Observations on the Application of Smart Pigging on Transmission Pipelines," prepared for the Pipeline Safety Trust, September 5, 2005.
[24] Ibid., API Standard 1163.

It is the nature of production pipelines to load slug as liquid/solid carryover cycles the system. This, as well as the additional corrosion risks discussed in Section III, are some of the fundamental differences between design/operation of production and transmission pipelines. Theoretically, flaw growth plots similar to those for corrosion (Figures 5 and 7), can be developed for sharp edged pipeline flaws such as third party damage gouges. The tests, theories, and many years of field verification that evolved for corrosion failure tools on pipelines have yet to be clearly developed for the sharp edged flaws. Corrosion anomalies tend to have varying thickness that do not concentrate the stresses in a manner such as that associated with sharp edge flaws (gouges). A fracture mechanics model developed for steel pipe would take on a similar appearance to that of Figures 5 and 7, with flaw sizes of sharp edge permitted at the same pressure level being much smaller than that for corrosion. For a given pressure, a pipeline can tolerate a corrosion flaw but not necessarily the same size (depth and length) sharp edge gouge anomaly. It is very important that any pipeline route take rational precautions to avoid and prevent possible third party damage on such a high-pressure pipeline that commands such a large potential impact zone.

Thicker pipe, even at the higher stress levels, does provide one definite benefit in regard to a specific type of third party damage threat. Damages where a hit results in a stress concentrator within a dent (i.e., dent with a gouge, crack, or corrosion). Dent with stress concentrators are not permitted in most codes or regulations as their time to failure are very unpredictable (they can fail at any time). Most third party damage on thick-walled pipe will probably result in a gouge rather then a gouge within a dent. The stress concentrator may not fail immediately, but such damage would be susceptible to fatigue cycling and possible failure that is still very unpredictable.

Lastly, a major issue of concern regarding third party damage, that of the waiver from the requirement to utilise a 0.3 design criteria (much thicker wall pipe) for road and railroad crossings. The pipeline is proposed to be constructed with a 0.72 design factor throughout the system, including road

> Road crossing loading calculations need to be adequately documented.

crossings. There are two major risks associated with crossings: 1) possible damage associated with third party activity that could hit and possibly gouge the pipeline as discussed above, and 2) abnormal loading associated with heavy traffic crossing the pipeline. Requirements to install a concrete warning barrier and warning tape appear adequate to address the first risk of concern. Usually, to protect from the second risk of concern, the pipeline is either encased or buried very deeply to spread the loading forces. We do not advise casing the pipe in this environment as casing can accelerate selective external corrosion. The operator needs to provide detailed loading calculations assuring that <u>each specific site crossing</u> will provide adequate safety margin from abnormal loading that could result in pipeline failure from crush or similar loading. Given the thickness of the pipe, road crossing abnormal loading should not be an area of concern, but this needs to be clearly demonstrated.

Remote Monitoring of Pipelines

Little mention is given in various public documents as to how this pipeline will be remotely operated or controlled. This is no surprise as most regulatory requirements do not address this issue competently, or even provide minimal guidance. There is an indication that the control centre for the pipeline will be at the Gas Processing Plant control room. A clear reading of this paper should raise new questions as to how this pipeline should be controlled, protected from overpressure, and monitored.

The Illusions of Leak Detection

Several studies concerning the Corrib pipeline have indicated a desire to improve safety performance and reduce risks by incorporating "sophisticated automatic leak detection" on this pipeline. While common sense would suggest an attempt at some form of leak detection on this system, we must caution that any credit for such a system is highly illusionary for this production pipeline. Despite claims that may be made by leak system manufacturers selling such systems, the likelihood of any of these systems identifying leaks in real time is nearly zero (the author can't rule out random luck accidentally flagging a release). We find claims, assertions, or inferences that any sophisticated automatic leak detection system operating on the Corrib pipeline will actually prevent casualties or fatalities near the pipeline to be without merit. For the record, the author has seen many "leak detection" systems and none has really worked reliably to date. An analysis of the long record of gas pipeline failures will prove the frustrations of trying to get a remote leak detection system to properly signal a real release on a highly compressed gas system (i.e., forget mass balance) without burdening the control room operator with a phalanx of false alarms that train operators to ignore alarms.

The truth of the matter is that for leaks (releases from fixed orifices as described in section IV – Understanding Pipeline Releases), the compressibility of the gas and the multiple phase operation of this production pipeline make leak discovery via remote monitoring extremely difficult if not impossible. It must also be stressed that this gas will be unodorised (the traditional method of alerting the public and neighborhood of possible signs of leaks on a pipeline). The only method that has a chance of determining gas leaks on this onshore pipeline is the tried and true method of walking the pipeline with an appropriate gas detector, and even this approach is not infallible and only detects possible leaks at the time of the survey.

> In any risk analysis no credit should be incurred for "automatic" leak detection on this system.

It is now important to discuss rupture releases and the inability of leak detection monitoring systems to reliably determine such massive releases. As incredible as this may appear, many in the pipeline industry do not easily understand or grasp this concept so the average layman can be forgiven for not comprehending this point at first review. Leak detection systems are not able to determine the high mass rate releases associated with ruptures in a gas pipeline in a timely manner. This is due to the many transient factors mentioned in Section IV such as the compressed nature of the gas, choke flow, and pipe hydraulic dynamics. As a result, the various critical signals don't get recognised by detection devices either upstream or downstream of the rupture in sufficient time to respond to a rupture and prevent fatalities within the zone. In fact, the number one method for detection of a gas pipeline rupture is a call in by observers who may witness such an event. Unfortunately, given the very large size of the rupture impact zone for this very unique pipeline, callers may not be nearby as those people near a rupture, in all probability, will be dead or dying. It has been suggested that the meter entering the Gas Processing Plant (at the end of the onshore pipeline) can be utilised to indicate a pipeline rupture on the onshore pipeline. Transient release calculations indicate the time it would take for such a clear indication to show up at the Gas Processing Plant, even at this relatively short distance, will be past the major and multiple fatality exposure time for a rupture event.

Any claims that mass balance can identify leaks or failures on this pipeline need to be seriously challenged. Even if one could accurately mass balance in and out of the pipeline there is no way that a correct accounting of the change in gas inventory could permit an accurate leak or rupture detection. This pipeline contains a highly compressible fluid operating in the triple phase region (solid/liquid/gas) with a pipeline diameter that seriously affects transient dynamics. Under our obligation to maintain objectivity and completeness, a meter at the Gas Processing Plant end of the pipeline may eventually suggest a possible rupture, but by the time this signal is indicated (it isn't immediate because of line hydraulics), acknowledged, and responded to by control centre personnel, in all probability the rupture cloud has ignited. Our intent is not to scare, but this is serious material being transported at very high pressures. Frankness is merited especially given the extreme inexperience evidenced in previous statements implying the effectiveness of leak detection to prevent fatalities.

VII. The Myth of Highest International Standards

Major Differences in International Standards

Several international standards have been reported and compared in an accompanying study related to the Corrib pipeline.[25] A reading of that study will leave the observer questioning if there really is a clear guideline standard for this pipeline. There should be no surprise about this confusion as many of these standards are in a state of flux and do not adequately address the very unique operation of the Corrib onshore pipeline. For example, none of the cited standards directly address the extreme pressure operation of the Corrib pipeline (e.g., the pressure is off the chart in various standards that attempt to quantify separation distances from dwellings).

> Proclamations claiming "highest international standards" carry very little weight and appear to be a public relations attempt to placate an inquiring public challenging or raising real issues of concern.

The author is often asked about which international pipeline standards are the best. We believe that no one standard is the best. Some standards are better in some areas, even leading edge in certain areas, and very incomplete in other areas. These differences, that can be very important, vary from country to country. One particular country's standards, even if they are "better" in certain areas, may not be applicable to a particular situation in another country as many factors may be different. It is a myth perpetuated by the industry that there are international standards out there that reign supreme, especially if a country permits risk analysis to waive even those minimum requirements that may have been developed through years of experience.

Highest international standard statements tend to create an illusion that can be very dangerous, especially if this illusion relies on misapplication of risk analysis techniques, or if the project team starts to believe their own myths that nothing will fail, and takes very unnecessary or unwise risks in their design approach to reduce costs.

A pipeline design only complying with minimum regulations needs to be carefully analysed and scrutinised. This is especially critical if the project is pushing technical boundaries such as being a "model one" or "off the chart" in the minimum standards. There is nothing that prevents an operator from exceeding any standard. By now it should be obvious to most readers that critical information regarding this project has not been disclosed, and maybe not even considered, and these important details need to be publicly discussed and the project's proposed design reevaluated. This is especially important given the many serious misrepresentations concerning this project as identified in this report. One other important point regarding international pipeline standards is that the physical laws governing prudent engineering approaches know no international boundaries.

The Standard Driving This Pipeline

The standard most often cited in various public documents for the Corrib pipeline is BS 8010 (circa 1992), a standard that has now gone out of date. Because of the need to restrict the length of this paper, the author will focus on the one major section of this code that appears to be driving the over focus on risk analysis or QRA. The BS 8010 code, subsection 2.4.2.4 states "Pipeline designed to operate outside the range of maximum operating pressure and pipe diameters shown in figure 2 may be acceptable provided a more detailed assessment of potential additional hazard is made in conjunction with a safety evaluation (see 2.3)."[26] Figure 2 is a chart of "Minimum distances from normally occupied buildings for methane (a category D substance.)" The chart only goes up to 100 Bar maximum operating pressure. Subsection 2.3

---

[25] Ibid., Andrew Johnson, "Corrib Gas Pipeline Project Report on Evaluation of Onshore Pipeline Design Code."
[26] Ibid., BS 8010.

outlines requirements of a safety evaluation and includes subsection 2.3.2 defining the minimum requirements needed to incorporate a "Risk Analysis."

Risk analyses to date for the Corrib onshore pipeline have failed to properly or adequately comply with the five basic minimum requirements defined in Standard BS 8010, subsection 2.3 (a through e) allowing risk analysis.

A comparison of the many key issues noted in this paper to previous QRAs for the Corrib pipeline will clearly demonstrate serious deficiencies, mischaracterisations, and/or misstatements in these prior efforts. The QRA approach needs to be seriously re-evaluated for this unique onshore, very high pressure, pipeline system.

Misperceptions and Misapplications of QRA

While it should now be obvious after reading the above section why there is so much focus on QRA for this particular proposed pipeline, additional comments concerning the QRA process need to be captured as a matter of public record. While this author has been very clear that risk analysis for the Corrib proposal has failed to meet the minimum requirements for a risk analysis defined in BS 8010, a brief commentary on several additional common errors observed in all too many risk analyses is necessary. Special attention should be given to any risk assessment that summarily dismisses specific failure cases as "not credible" without sufficient proof. The burden of substantiation should rest on the risk performer to demonstrate why such an event was not evaluated. The dismissal of events as "not credible" can be overly utilised to manoeuvre a risk analysis to a preordained conclusion. That is not the intent or purpose in standards that usually allow the use of this tool.

While a statistically based assessment of failure mode and frequency is required in some risk assessment approaches, all too often the statistical base does not represent the assets being evaluated. For example, utilising past pipeline databases for rupture frequency that include distribution as well as transmission pipelines seriously under represent the high stress pipeline failure frequency, as distribution pipelines don't rupture. Assuming a production pipeline has the same failure frequency from internal corrosion as a transmission pipeline also understates production pipeline statistics for failure, as transmission pipelines are usually not permitted to transport the more corrosive fluids associated with production pipelines. And lastly, we must comment that statistical approaches mainly focusing on past historical events or databases don't properly apply to first of their kind or model one infrastructure. History is a very poor predictor of future failures for such new, complex, at-risk systems that may be pushing the envelope. Ask the NASA launch management team on the last Challenger launch about the follies of rushing to a pre-ordained objective based on past history prediction calls. Quite simply, it should be obvious by now that risk analysis is very inappropriate for this most unusual, first of its kind, application in Ireland.

VIII. Why the Corrib Gas Must be Treated

The proposed onshore pipeline route presents the greatest risk to population. The Gas Processing Plant placement greatly influences risks associated with the onshore pipeline.

By now the reader should be starting to appreciate that the production gas from the Corrib field creates additional risks on a steel pipeline (see Figure 4, 5, and 7 for just the corrosion issues). The gas is not acceptable to be transported in gas transmission or distribution pipelines. This begs the question of why would such a high-pressure production pipeline be placed in the close vicinity of population. The bulk of the previous discussion has focused on the pipeline for very critical, and by now obvious, reasons. Pipelines can have very large impact footprints in close proximity to people. From a safety perspective, an onshore Corrib pipeline rupture presents the greatest safety risk to the population from a failure because a pipeline rupture will release many tons more material in close proximity to people than a Gas Processing Plant release (the plant equipment has very limited inventory in comparison to the pipeline). The Gas Processing Plant, as presently configured, has additional requirements (such as process safety management or Hazid) that tend to limit the impact of equipment failure to areas on or close to the plant site. A more detailed discussion of the Gas Processing Plant and how its location influences various risk factors on the onshore pipeline is now, however, appropriate.

The Major Contaminants

Liquids (hydrocarbon and water) must be removed from the wet production gas as such liquids not only add to corrosion potential but also create internal loading stresses on pipelines that can be quite high, especially when these accumulated liquids are driven by the high pressures expected for this field and production pipeline. In addition, unique contaminants such as excess CO_2 or H_2S must be treated if they are present in appreciable quantities that might affect transmission or distribution pipeline systems or customer safety. The original design for the Gas Processing Plant includes no removal for CO_2 or H_2S contaminants as the current field apparently, at least at the start of production, is not expected to contain these contaminants in quantities requiring treatment to protect downstream pipelines.

Key Equipment

A simplified flow diagram of the terminal proposed at the end of the Corrib pipeline is indicated in Figure 18. The bulk of this equipment is for simple liquid removal for elemental gas drying.

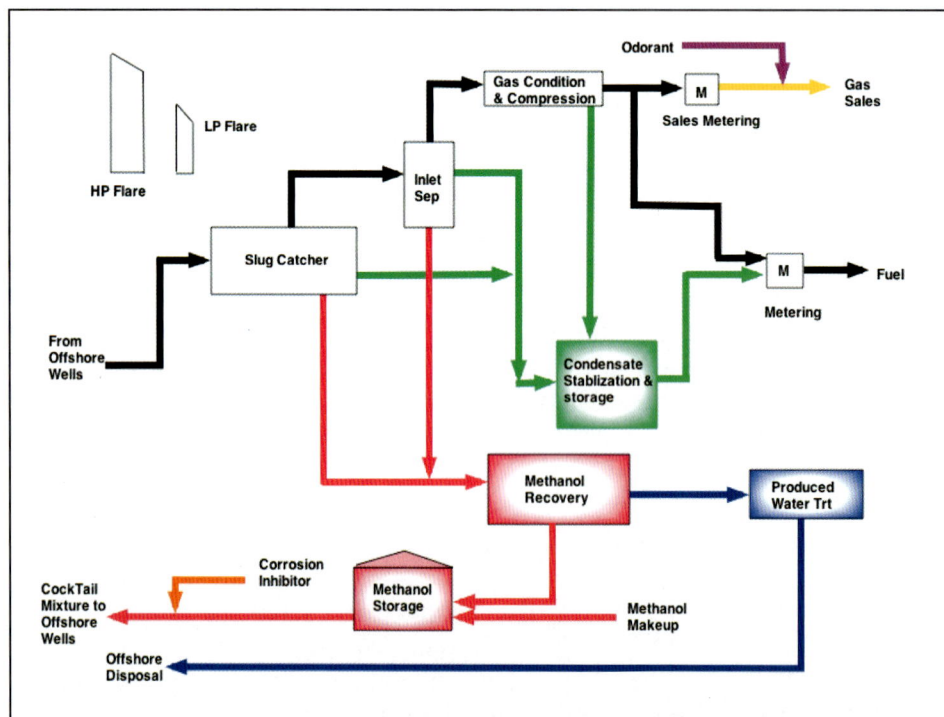

FIGURE 18. CORRIB PROPOSED ONSHORE GAS PROCESSING PLANT BASIC PROCESS FLOW SCHEME

Some minor complexity has been added to separate hydrocarbon liquid from water for fuel use or sale. Depending on the quality of the material from the gas field, a typical gas processing plant usually incorporates phase separation (gas/liquid/solid), additional gas drying as warranted, specialised gas treatment and/or liquid separation (i.e., removal of natural gas liquids, or NGLs). Additional treatment can involve the removal of various impurities and gas contaminants such as CO_2 or sulphur that are not part of the Corrib design to date.

For the Corrib plant, additional minor complexity has been added to process methanol recovered for recycle and reuse in the production pipeline. Some minor storage facilities have also been incorporated. We would classify this proposal as a low to moderately low complex gas processing or treating facility. Much of the stored chemicals are not required in gas transmission or distribution pipeline operations but are intended solely for the gas production line operation.

Two flares, a high-pressure (HP) and a low-pressure (LP) flare, are proposed and we have not indicated their specific tie-in points in the facility as that has not been defined in previously reviewed documents. The HP flare will be a tall stack unit designed for a production line capacity of 350 MMSCFD. The LP flare is apparently a much smaller capacity unit (8 MMSCFD) intended for minor blow down or purging during maintenance of facility equipment. For safety reasons, we would advise the use of limited flaring over cold venting (discussed in the next section) given the capability of venting to generate heavier than air vapours that can produce catastrophic events in the area should a release get away from the operator.

> Cold venting should be avoided in prudent gas processing plant design.

Separation and treatment often entail producing constituents for sale, disposal, or re-injection into the producing fields if sale/disposal/use is not viable or economical. The specific plant design, complexity, and location will depend on the quality of the gas produced from the field(s) and the local demands and obstacles. The boxes in white in Figure 18 convey the simple processes involved in phase separation to produce sales gas. The other coloured boxes are additions the operator has selected to improve field efficiency (i.e., profitability) such as methanol recovery and recycle.

FIGURE 19. GAS PLANT SITE LOOKING TOWARD CARROWMORE LAKE

Documents also indicate that additional complexity concerning refrigeration components and storage (i.e., propane) suggest that additional hydrocarbon liquid recovery can be anticipated, either as the gas field ages or additional fields are brought into production.[27] This additional infrastructure would still be regarded as moderate, even if additional bulk storage is required, such as for propane refrigeration. It is important to recognise that this may not be the only production pipeline that might utilise this plant site.

A processing plant, while apparently not specifically defined in the BS 8010 standard, is a combination of process plant/treating, and storage facilities related to a gas pipeline operation.[28]

---

[27] Ibid., Inspector Report to An Bord Pleanála.

33

The term "Terminal" apparently is also not defined in the standard, but by reference to the same standard BS 8010 Figure 1, this proposed plant facility is not a "Terminal" in the strictest interpretation. The term Refinery within the industry is usually reserved for the much more complex series of processes intended for crude oil or liquid hydrocarbon processing facilities. We understand that Irish law may carry a specific meaning of the word "Refinery," but this author is not familiar with this specific legal definition. We would thus characterise the facility at the end of the Corrib onshore pipeline as a Gas Processing Plant. The land footprint for this site would suggest that other major infrastructure is under consideration for this site as the footprint appears much greater than that needed for the basic simple Corrib design needs.

Cold Venting

An issue that can play a pivotal role in onshore siting decisions for a gas processing plant is the matter of cold venting. Cold venting is the release of gas (usually primarily methane) out a gas processing plant vent stack to atmosphere in such a manner that it is not burned. The theory is that the lighter than air gases rise up into the atmosphere. While most streams are mainly methane, which is lighter than air, serious safety concerns appear when heavier than air components or toxic chemicals start to show up in the gas stream than might be vented. Cold venting can be very dangerous, not only for plant personnel but also the neighbouring population. Depending on the composition of the material in the gas stream, especially if a plant is located on a site in proximity to people, dispersion can send heavier than air gas components to ground level with tragic results.

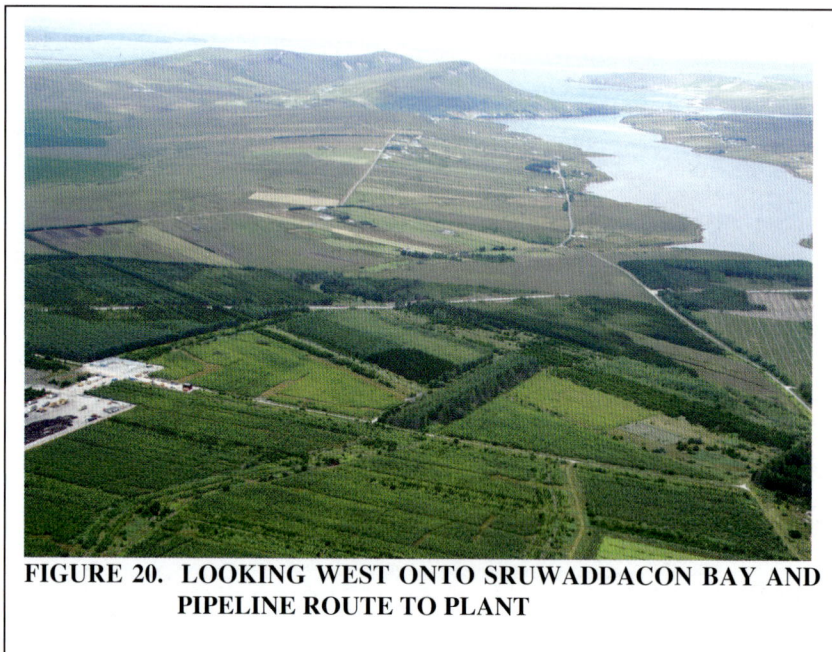

FIGURE 20. LOOKING WEST ONTO SRUWADDACON BAY AND PIPELINE ROUTE TO PLANT

Cold venting is usually the by-product of remote oil field design, but an over focus on capital reduction for gas field development (i.e., to boost rate of return) can drive a company to select cold venting over wiser alternatives that require additional equipment. Cold venting should not make sense in a world where energy prices are increasing, but it can still occur because of the economics and investment philosophies of particular companies. Failure to properly restrict the option of cold venting should be regarded as a serious deficiency and prevented in any modern processing plant design and approval. Several responsible governments and world agencies have incorporated practices to discourage cold venting in their energy field development.

Flaring Issues

Flaring is the intentional burning of gas (in a flare stack) before it is released to the atmosphere (forming combustion byproducts such as CO_2, NO_X and other compounds). Flaring is usually preferred over cold venting as several safety issues associated with cold venting as mentioned

---

[28] Ibid., BS8010: Section 2.8, "Figure 1. Extent of pipeline systems for conveying oil and gas which are covered by this Section." 1992.

above are avoided.[29] The major issue with flaring is when plant operators flare excessively, either because of poor plant design or poor equipment maintenance, that results in frequent equipment breakdown causing long duration flaring. Excessive or frequent flaring, in addition to wasting a valuable commodity, can contribute to combustion pollutants, excessive noise (large flares can make a lot of noise), and light pollution. Excessive flaring can now be easily eliminated by proper gas plant design, maintenance, and investment encouraged by proper governmental permitting procedures.

More to Come

If the Gas Processing Plant were the only equipment to be placed at the onshore site it would be fairly easy to recommend its placement as, relatively speaking, the equipment depicted in Figure 18 is fairly straightforward. The plant is limited in complexity and can be easily judged as to its safety by a basic review of: 1) a plant layout drawing to review major equipment placement and separation, 2) various simple P& ID's, and 3) an analysis of the HAZID.[30] The footprint for a simple gas plant is not the large size currently projected (see Figure 3, large red quadrangle), suggesting that other processes may be in future schemes. Given the lack of clarity related to this project to date and demonstrated by this report, it is understandable that the local citizens have little confidence in denials concerning future expectations for this site. It is beyond the scope of this report to analyse all possible additional infrastructures that could be sited, but it would not be beyond reason to assume that an oil refinery would be desired in close proximity to a reliable gas source. It is usually the responsibility of local governments overseeing land use planning to properly communicate the possible future infrastructure that a new energy supply brings to the area. Future site plans or alternatives for the proposed onshore facility should be clearly communicated.

IX. Is the Gas Processing Plant Site Driving the Pipeline Route?

There is a strong appearance that the availability of the Gas Processing Plant land site may be driving the decision to route a production pipeline in an unwise location. Given the choice to site the Gas Processing Plant, the operators have proclaimed that the proposed route for the onshore pipeline is the best route available and other alternatives have serious conflicts or challenges.[31] A quick scan of the countryside would clearly indicate that there are many ways to get to the Gas Processing Plant without utilising the particular route selected by the operator.

In Pipeline Routing, the Shortest path is Seldom the Cheapest

The burden of proof should fall on the pipeline operator to clearly explain and demonstrate that alternative routes to the plant were adequately explored and the reasons for their rejection clearly presented and properly communicated.

Apparently, once the Gas Processing Plant site was chosen, the pipeline route near the bay appears to have been selected as the shortest and easiest path to get to the terminal. Ironically, as seen from Figure 3, this route places a very unique high-pressure production pipeline in close proximity to population. We cannot stress the importance of getting this highly unique production pipeline away from people, not just dwellings. As the public becomes more informed about the lack of clear information about this system, the delays in this project will cost more than any original cost savings ever proposed for this unwise route selection. This is an often observed phenomenon in pipeline routing decisions. Pipeline operators choose the shortest or easiest path based on perceived cost savings only to discover the folly of such

---

[29] Flaring is often incorporated as a safety design to protect processing plant and personnel. In these modern design schemes such plants rarely flare excessively for long periods of time as such flaring is only required during major plant equipment malfunction or breakdown.

[30] P&IDs are pipe and instrument drawings, while HAZID stands for a hazard identification process required for facilities falling under process safety management.

[31] Ibid., Inspector Report to An Bord Pleanála.

unwise tactics. An informed public becomes wise to their manoeuvres, and delays or changes the project in ways that quickly consume any cost savings that the original easiest path ever hoped to realise. The shortest pipeline path, especially if an unwise selection, is seldom the cheapest.

Land Use Planning

Land use planning as it relates to future activity near infrastructure is a critically important activity, not only when determining pipeline routes, but also for selecting other facilities such as gas processing plants or other complex infrastructure they may attract, such as refineries. The importance of keeping certain threats away from high-pressure pipelines that can release extremely large inventories of material should be obvious by now to the reader of this report. What is less understood is the importance of understanding the infrastructure that may be associated with gas plant siting. Ironically, from a safety perspective, these other non pipeline facilities usually, but not always, fall under the regulatory regime of process safety management.

Process safety management is a basket of requirements that assure that a company's management approach meets certain basic minimum process requirements and checks and balances to avoid potential failures, especially large catastrophic events associated with certain plant assets. It is one of the requirements of process safety management, sometimes referred to as process hazard management, to carefully review plant siting, design, and operation issues when chemical inventories exceed a certain capacity. Unfortunately, process safety management processes usually aren't required of pipelines. Typically a process safety audit requires an evaluation of the potential for various worse case events to leave the plant site. Please note that such a review does not involve an evaluation of environmental issues or concerns, and usually doesn't capture the impact or additional risk such a facility places on the pipeline.

X. Advice for Government, Public, and Regulatory Authorities

It is beyond the scope of this paper to pass judgment as to how a critical energy supply should be developed for Ireland. That is an issue best left to the Irish government and its citizens and the companies they choose to do business with. It is, however, clearly within the scope of this report to make observations as to the correctness of technical information related to this project and various options.

Various Offshore vs. Onshore Options

There are three basic fundamental processing option schemes for the Corrib gas field. The lengthy but very professional Inspector's Report should serve as an important information resource to explore these options in more detail if the reader is so inclined.[32] Several important factors (pros and cons) for each option are summarised in Table 1 for the reader's consideration. These options are briefly summarised as follows and are not intended to be an exhaustive list:

Option 1 Deep Water Offshore Processing Platform Located at Corrib Field

This scheme places a deepwater platform in water (350metres) with very harsh Atlantic weather conditions approximately 80 kilometres off the west coast of Ireland. Gas processing would be included on the platform and a gas transmission pipeline would run to landfall. This is similar to earlier traditional North Sea processing schemes.

---

[32] An Bord Pleanála, "Inspector's Report on Gas Terminal at Bellagelly South, Bellanaboy Bridge, Belmullet, Co. Mayo," signed by Kevin Moore and dated April 2003.

Option 2 Shallow Water Processing Platform with Processing Near Shore

Similar to Option 1 except the platform is moved closer to the Irish coast where it could be fixed to the ocean floor in shallow water and with much fewer challenges (and costs) than the deep water site. This option is similar to many traditional fixed offshore platforms across the world located in shallow water. Production pipeline from Corrib subsea wells would be routed to the offshore processing plant via a subsea production pipeline. A shorter transmission pipeline would be needed to make landfall.

Option 3 Onshore Processing Plant

A subsea production pipeline with a suitably routed onshore production pipeline would be placed in a proper location route to a suitably placed onshore gas processing plant.

TABLE 1. BASIC CORRIB GAS FIELD DEVELOPMENT OPTIONS

Option	Pros	Cons
Option 1 Deep Water Offshore Processing Platform Located at Corrib Field	1. Out of sight from land. 2. Safest for local communities. 3. No real environmental risk to communities. 4. Much lower transmission pipeline safety risk vs. higher production pipeline risks.	1. Most expensive by a wide margin. 2. Legitimate safety concerns at challenging platform site. 3. Potential offshore environmental risks. 4. Serious delay in field startup/development.
Option 2 Shallow Water Processing Platform with Processing Near Shore	1. Safest for local communities. 2. Much lower transmission pipeline safety risk vs. higher production pipeline risks.	1. Possible sight pollution from land. 2. More potential coastal pollution. 3. Still costly but much cheaper than option 1. 4. Shorter delay in field startup/development.
Option 3 Onshore Processing Plant	1. Cheapest option. 2. Lowest worker safety concerns. 3. Limited delay in field startup, development.	1. Most safety risks to communities. 2. Most environmental risk to communities. 3. Very limited local confidence in present proposal.

The simple comments in Table 1 focus on several fundamental factors: aesthetics, safety, environment, and economics. The reader can probably come up with additional factors, but these basic factors will raise enough discussion for the various players on a general level. How this project proceeds will be influenced by some combination of the approach decision makers take in prioritising at least these factors into their approval process. For example, the operator may tend to over focus on the economic factors (which usually aren't made public) at the expense of safety. Local citizens may tend to place a higher priority on aesthetics or quality of life issues at the expense of more economic considerations, especially if they don't realise any economic benefit while incurring all the perceived risks. Any project of this nature or magnitude requires proper communication, rational compromise, and appropriate balance. This can only occur if all parties bring to the table a willingness to discuss and agree on key fundamental facts, a process difficult to achieve in an atmosphere of deception or distortion. It is hoped that one of the objectives of this report is to get key leveraging facts on the table to allow parties to move constructively forward.

Dangers Associated with Retrofitting New Processes Onto Old Sites

All too often lately land that has been determined to be unsuitable has been made available, especially from governments who are looking for a quick way to unload a poor site on the next owner. Sometimes this bargain works out for all parties. Too often, however, cash strapped governments unload these sites in exchange for years of trouble for themselves and their constituents. Such fools' bargains end up being anything but a bargain for all. Governments typically answer to the people and it usually difficult to hide a bad arrangement that only gets worse with time. Bargain land sites that are inappropriate for their new use seldom end up saving money as retrofits or complications increase cost or seriously delay projects, while increasing the likelihood of system failure due to increased complexity from various quick retrofit fixes that should never have occurred. If a fundamental site is poor for its newly selected purposes, expect many delays in project schedule that can eat up profitability (and rate of return) because of the time value of money.

The Failure and Misapplication of QRA

In a more complex society, risk analysis or QRAs can be a valuable tool to ensure proper resources are allocated to a project. While a QRA can serve as a valuable tool, one should be on the lookout to determine if this approach is being misapplied to hide or confuse the real risk of a poor project approach or design. Too often QRAs, even those permitted in regulatory standards, can be manipulated or biased to serve a preordained objective, which is not the purpose of such an important tool. Warning signs that signal problems in QRA approaches are: 1) the inability to clearly define or commit to the project's base case and its important boundary parameters, 2) an undercurrent permeating the analysis that equipment can't fail, causing serious bias in the outcome, 3) limited evaluation indicated by a preponderance of too many "not credible case" determinations without sufficient backup documents proving such determinations, 4) misapplication of historical statistics that don't apply to the project conditions, 5) failure to recognise that new cutting edge applications are beyond the bounds of historical statistics and that failure mechanisms may thus take on new forms, 6) overemphasis on component failure that ignores the more likely probability that the system will be driven to failure by linked system complexity injected from quick fixes, 7) inconsistency in outlining a project's objectives, 8) an over-emphasis in presentations on low probability even though the consequences are enormous (like severe loss of life), 9) a sense that the analysis is failing to remain neutral, and 10) failure to tell the truth. There may be differences of opinion, but certain fundamental physical issues are hard to dispute once they have been uncovered. If too many of the above are showing up in a risk analysis for a project, the risk analysis approach needs to be rejected.

> The previously discussed issues of cold venting and/or excess flaring are a classic example of a short-term fixation (rewards the operator) that may not be in the best interest of a country's energy resource (waste of salable energy).

Environmental Factors and Long Term Effects

It is not the objective of this paper to perform a detailed analysis of the possible environmental factors associated with this project. It should be obvious by now, however, that many issues have been identified that any decision concerning this project must include. Any environmental analysis that fails to address the long-term ramifications on its surroundings would be seriously deficient. All too often the message on the benefits of a project focuses only on the short-term issues (especially on QRA), while ignoring the long-term costs that are very real and may easily outweigh the short term benefits by orders of magnitude. This is an outcome of today's misinformation society where the rush to produce short-term results tends to overlook or understate the very real costs associated with the long-term impacts. And, of course, a major issue to all players is what the proposed gas plant site would look like a decade from now. A possible industrial complex can have serious implications for the area that may not be in line with its citizens' intentions.

Lastly, we have focused on the terrible consequences associated with fire/explosion from a pipeline failure. We need to not lose sight that there are pipeline failures where fire would not occur such as leaks and even some ruptures. Fire, while thermally destructive, tends to eliminate via combustion those chemicals that might be associated with future composition changes. The nature of releases without fire should not be toxic or have long term environmental effects that cannot be remediated, provided the composition of the gas transported in the pipeline has not changed markedly. The unknown in this prediction is the nature of the gas that may be produced or discovered in the future, especially if new fields introduce more toxic compounds, such as H_2S. It is advisable that this should also be considered in land use planning when choosing an appropriate site. In addition, while the production pipeline may not introduce long-term environmental effects, its failure could cause a release of the utility pipeline with its hydraulic, methanol/corrosion inhibitor cocktail lines. This cocktail mix could be a special problem to water given the tenacity for the cocktail to seek and hold onto water. Limited spill volume from the utility line would probably restrict the size and effects associated with long term environmental damage provided such releases are quickly addressed. Generally, the nature of a gas pipeline and its gas processing facility is limited on its long term environmental impacts compared to more industrialised facilities such as oil refineries. This does not mean that an improperly designed or operated gas plant cannot cause environmental damage, but by its nature a properly designed, operated, and maintained facility is limited on its long term impact to the environment including air, water, and nearby population.

Third Worlding and the Misuse of Land

Within the industry a term has become popular lately: "third worlding." In this context, third worlding means to unwisely allow use of land for purposes that, in all probability, will result in severe loss of life. However, the country's government places so little real value on such loss, that corporations, or for that matter, governments are willing to take the risk of massive catastrophic failure, usually for perceived short term gain. Now there is still a lot of open land in the world where very high risk corporate adventures would not place large populations at risk. Unfortunately, the reader can probably bring to mind examples where short term gain has driven governments to take foolish risks. Look for indications of over application of QRA to hide such poor risk approaches. Someone once told the author that risk management was the tool for the few in power to impose their will on the many. If I recall correctly, the person credited with that quote was talking about the Three Mile Island nuclear power plant, before the meltdown!

Liability and Financial Impacts of Poor Risk Management

In keeping with the theme that risk analysis may not be properly applied to a project, especially to an effort of this magnitude, each country and its citizens must decide the liability/reward equation for its interest. One of the factors showing up in too many countries is the phenomenon where fines or penalties are relatively small or inconsequential for inappropriate actions as compared to huge profit potential. This big profit/small fine factor can drive decision makers to take unwise risks that are not captured in a risk analysis, for example. From an international corporation's perspective, the risks are worth taking as the liabilities are perceived as small. In analyzing many failures in energy infrastructure, this author has observed in too many situations, how a group of very smart people in a company or government, can end up doing ill-advised things that as individuals they would never do. Liability risks can serve as a proper check and balance on such unwise processes to ensure businesses and governments stay professional and avoid recklessness. A question that needs to be answered by the citizens of Ireland concerning the present proposal is whether Irish law would permit legitimate actions for criminal negligence that caused serious environmental damage or loss of life. Some countries have such laws and effective processes in place to enforce them. This issue can be leveraging if risk management is applied in countries with few or illusionary liability risks that are not just reserved for third world countries.

XI. Conclusion and Recommendations

It should be fairly obvious by now that past information on this project has been less than complete. Much of this information appears to be of a propaganda nature intended to spin public relations to an ill informed or misinformed public or government. In today's information age this is a tactic fraught with risks as the deceptions are uncovered.

Regarding the proposed onshore pipeline route, serious challenges should be raised as to any risk analysis that fails to adequately address the issues raised by the production pipeline, as the thermal impact zones for this very unique high pressure pipeline are quite large with a high probability of mortality. It is the opinion of the author that the risks of the pipeline have been considerably understated. Various critical commitments that would ensure that the pipeline would not fail have not been clearly demonstrated or obligated, a serious indication that in all probability risk assessment is not appropriate for this project. If the Gas Processing Plant site location were to remain as proposed, we advise a reroute of the proposed pipeline incorporating safety buffer zones of 200 metres for dwellings and at least 400 metres for unsheltered individuals.

The recommendation concerning the placement of the onshore Gas Process Plant is more complicated by the unknowns associated with potential future complexities or possible additions that have not been defined in this project. The placement of a relatively simple Gas Process Plant onshore at the end of a production pipeline would not in itself create an unwarranted safety risk to the local public from the plant. Placement of a Gas Process Plant on a shallow offshore platform would substantially reduce production pipeline rupture impact zones associated with specific pipeline design modifications. A transmission pipeline from such an offshore facility could be operated at lower pressures, move much higher quality gas, and permit appropriate cleaning and smart pigging programs that would reduce the potential impact zone associated with a gas transmission pipeline failure. The final decision on the Gas Process Plant site placement rests with the citizens. It is hoped that this report permits all parties to shift into a more responsible dialogue and reach a more informed and balanced decision on this critical matter.

XII. Bibliography

AEA Technology, "Independent Review of Onshore Pipeline Quantified Risk Assessment for the Corrib Field Development," dated June 2005.

Allseas for Enterprise Oil, "Onshore Pipeline Quantified Risk Assessment, Corrib Field Development Project, Version D," dated Feb 2002.

Allseas for Enterprise Oil, "Onshore Pipeline Quantified Risk Assessment, Corrib Field Development Project, Version E," dated July, 2002.

Allseas, "Onshore Pipeline Quantified Risk Assessment, Corrib Field Development Project, Version F," dated April, 2005.

American Society of Mechanical Engineers, ASME B31.8, "Gas Transmission and Distribution Pipeline Systems," 2004 edition.

American Society of Mechanical Engineers, ASME B31.8S, "Managing System Integrity of Gas Pipelines," 2004 edition.

American Petroleum Institute, API Standard 1163, "In-line Inspection Systems Qualification Standard," First Edition, August, 2005.

Bilio, M. and Kinsman, P.R., "Thermal Radiation Criteria Used in Pipeline Risk Assessment," Pipes & Pipelines International, 1997.

BPA Report for PAD, DCMNR, "Corrib Gas Field Development – QRA Review," dated May 2005.

British Standard Institute BS 8010, "British Standard Code of Practice for Pipelines, Part 1. Pipelines on Land: General, 1989.

British Standard Institute BS 8010, "Code of Practice for Pipelines, Part 2. Pipelines on Land: Design, Construction and Installation, Section 2.8 Steel for Oil and Gas," 1992.

British Standard Institute PD 8010-1:2004, "Code of Practice for Pipelines, Part 1. Steel Pipelines on Land," 2004.

Eiber, Robert J., "Prediction of Corrib Pipeline Life for External and Internal Corrosion," September, 2005.

Eisenberg, N.A., Lynch, C.J. and Breeding, R.J., "Vulnerability Model: A Simulation System for Assessing Damage Resulting from Marine Spills," Environmental Control Report CG-D-136-75, 1975.

Environmental Impact Statement, "Bellanboy Bridge Terminal" Section 4 the Proposed Development," Enterprise Energy Ireland Ltd.

Inspector's Report to An Bord Pleanala, "Gas Terminal at Bellagelly South, Bellanaboy Bridge, Belmullet, Co. Mayo," dated April, 2003.

Institute of Gas Engineers, "Steel Pipelines for High Pressure Gas Transmission. Recommendation on Transmission and Distribution Practice," IGE/TD/1 Edition 3, 1993.

IS 328, "Code and Practice for the Design and Installation of Gas Transmission Pipelines," 2002.

Gas Research Institute, "A Model for Sizing High Consequence Areas Associated with Natural Gas Pipelines," prepared by C-FER Technologies, October, 2000.

Gas Research Institute, "Remote and Automatic Main Line Valve Technology Assessment," Final Report July, 1995.

Health and Safety Authority, "Land-use Planning Advice for Mayo County Council In Relation to the Application By Shell E&P Ireland Limited to Construct a Facility At Bellanaboy Bridge, Co. Mayo," dated April 8, 2004.

Hymes, I, "The Physiological and Pathological Effects of Thermal Radiation," Systems Reliability Directorate, Report SRD, R275, Culcheth, Warrington, UK, 1983.

Johnston, Andrew, "Corrib Gas Pipeline Project – Report on Evaluation of Onshore Pipeline Design Code," dated March 28, 2002.

Kuprewicz, Richard B., "Preventing Pipeline Releases," prepared for the Washington City County Pipeline Safety Consortium, July 22, 2003.

Kuprewicz, Richard B., "Observations on the Application of Smart Pigging on Transmission Pipelines," prepared for the Pipeline Safety Trust, September, 2005.

National Transportation Safety Board Pipeline Accident Report, "Natural Gas Pipeline Rupture and Fire Near Carlsbad, New Mexico August 19, 2000," NTSB/PAR-03/01, adopted February 11, 2003.

NORSAK Standards M-506, "CO_2 Corrosion Rate Calculation Model," Rev 2, June, 2005 at web site: www.standard.no/imaker.exe?id=10405.

PM Group Report, "Corrib Gas Field Quantified Risk Assessment – Executive Summary," dated May, 2005.

Shell Exploration and Production Letter to Mr. J Sheeran, Health and Safety Authority, dated April 6, 2004.
University of Tulsa Erosion/Corrosion Research Center, "CO2 Corrosion Research at the E/CRC Current Research Projects" web site: www.ecrc.utulsa.edu/crproj.htm.